LETTERS
to
LORI

"Little Girl Lost"

by
MARCIA MCALLISTER

Letters to Lori "Little Girl Lost"
ISBN 1453772383
© Copyright 2010 by Marcia McAllister
Palm Harbor, Florida

Illustrations and Cover Design by Maxine McClanahan
Covington, Georgia

Editing by Carol D. Witcher
Covington, Georgia

Published by Beacon of HOPE Publishing

Dedication

To my precious daughter,
Lori Lynn... a.k.a.   Lori Jane... Jello Jones...

You, of course, are the inspiration... and the reason for this book. It is all about you, daughter. It is your life story... it is your struggle... your decisions... your priorities... your mistakes... and your pain! It is also the story of all of us who love you so much... who see so much good in you... who see your potential and all that you can become in God.

Yes, we all see what a life of drug addiction has done to you... but we also see ahead and hope and believe that God is doing a wonderful work in you... that He always has had you in the palm of His hand... and that He, along with all of us... love you so very much!

We know that this is your time to take all the blessings that God has for you. This is your time to sort it all out and know that God has a wonderful plan for your life.

These words are for you, my daughter:

Isaiah 42:6-7: "I AM THE LORD, I HAVE CALLED YOU IN RIGHTEOUSNESS, I WILL ALSO HOLD YOU BY THE HAND AND WATCH OVER YOU, I WILL APPOINT YOU AS A COVENANT TO THE PEOPLE, AS A LIGHT TO THE NATIONS, TO

OPEN BLIND EYES, TO BRING OUT PRISONERS FROM THE DUNGEON, AND THOSE WHO DWELL IN DARKNESS FROM THE PRISON."

May you know the joy of your salvation... the fulfillment of your purpose upon this earth... and the desire to accomplish all that God has ordained for you!

YOUR MOM... who loves you so very much!

LETTERS TO LORI "Little Girl Lost"
Marcia McAllister
2010 First Edition

Acknowledgments

I want to thank all of you out there that have been a prayer support to me and my family through all these years of dealing with the pain of Lori's addiction. There are so many of you that know this story... know our struggles... know the pain that we have all experienced. So many of our family members have been a part of many of these events in Lori's life. My sisters, Jan and Karen... their husbands and families... and of course, my parents, Bill and Dorothy Wagner... have always been there for us through it all. My thanks to Lori's Dad, Allan, and his family, also, for their tireless efforts through these difficult years. So often all of these have helped in huge ways... and we are all so grateful for the support that they have shown.

My two sons, Ryan and Marc, have always been such a blessing to me through all of this. Ryan's wife, Elizabeth and their children... my precious grandchildren, Rylan, Chase and Justin have experienced the pain and agony many times of difficult situations with Lori. They have always been there... always tried to help... always understood that this is a way of life that Lori has chosen... but that we must pray for her and help as much as we can and believe God for the miracle transformation that we all know He has wanted to do in her life. Marc continues to be a strength to all of us... a wonderful listening ear... and a prayer warrior like Ryan and Elizabeth have been for Lori all these years.

Many thanks to all of you in our ministry that continue to pray for all of us... especially holding Lori in your prayers for so many years now. May you be blessed for your continued support and encouragement to us.

And, of course, there is precious Levi Jay... Lori's son. He is such a wonderful little guy, who loves his Mommy so much. May he continue to grow into all that God has planned for his life.

As always, my sincere thanks must go to Carol and Maxine of McWit Creative Works in Georgia... my publishing and editing team. This project would be so difficult without you. God brought you into my life and ministry in 2004 and the generosity of your time and talents is demonstrated in this work... once again. May God bless you so abundantly for all the hard work that has gone into this new manuscript.

May God get all the praise and glory for not only the writing of this account... but especially, we believe, for all the good that will come from it to so many. Yes, there is HOPE in the midst of the struggle!

In His love and for His glory,
Marcia McAllister

TABLE

OF

CONTENTS

TABLE OF CONTENTS

TABLE OF CONTENTS (continued)

CHAPTER ONE
S𝒿unned and Shocked!

April 28, 2010

Well, it has happened... the dreaded phone call has just come in! I've been anticipating this particular phone call for a few months now. Maybe that knowledge... that this phone call might happen... should have been enough to prepare me for the drastic piece of news that I have just received. Yes, maybe I should have prepared myself more for this outcome. But, evidently I haven't prepared enough.

Immediately the tears well up in my eyes. I can't control them. They are now cascading down my face like a waterfall. I can barely see to drive. I really should pull over... shouldn't I? But I can't ... I just keep driving. I must do something... I must not feel this intense pain right now. I have appointments to keep. I'm a busy realtor, you know. I have people waiting on me. I am booked up for the next several

1

hours. How can I even spare the time to pull the car to the side of the road to let the tears flow freely? Now, they are pouring out of my eyes. I can't think straight. I can't imagine what she is thinking right now. How is she feeling? Is she scared? She has to be scared... and shocked and stunned. Doesn't she? She has to feel all of this. I know she has to feel what I feel this moment... or does she?

And then it all hits me... it hits me so hard I can hardly process my thoughts. The knowledge that my beautiful, talented daughter has just received a five year prison sentence hits me... it hits me so hard that I feel that I have just been punched hard in the stomach. I am crying... I am alone... I am afraid for her... I am hurting so much I can hardly keep on driving... but I do. I manage to pull it together just enough to finally pick up the phone and try to reach both of my sons. I need them now... I need their reassurance that this will all turn out for the good for their sister... my daughter... my precious daughter, Lori.

Moments later my oldest son, Ryan sees that I have tried to reach him in this busy work day and calls back. He didn't know the news that I have just heard. He also is shocked... stunned, he says. Yes, he saw this coming... knew this day would probably come... but yes, he is almost speechless, too. He tells me that he has always wondered if he would get a phone call in the middle of the night that someone has found her body... that she has overdosed and is no longer here on this earth with us. He has wondered... is this the year that Lori will leave us... leave us for good? He tells me all of this... as I continue to cry... cry into his ear... pour out my pain to him... my firstborn. He volunteers to call his Dad... my ex-husband and find out what happened in court that morning. He will call me back... just as soon as he reaches his Dad.

I sit now in a parking lot... overcome by grief... overcome by the continued feelings of uncertainty. What will life be like for my daughter for the next few years? What horrors will she experience? Will she be safe in prison? Will she cry herself to sleep at night? Will she be overcome with guilt and dismay? Will she really come to regret the choices she has made for so many years? Will she recover from this experience that she is about to live through....for so long? Will she be able to start over... have a fresh start... will she come to her senses? Will she change...really change?

All of this is yet to unfold before us... We don't know how she will handle this prison sentence. Will it make her... or break her? Will it give her time to really be clean and finally think straight and make quality decisions? Will it give her a chance to process all her pain of the past... all her wrong decisions? Or will she become hardened... more rebellious... more determined to live the way she wants to live with no apparent care or concern for those who love her so very much. Which way will all this turn out?

God, Lori is in your hands. One more time I give her to you this day. I can't change her... I can't coerce her into making the right decisions for her life. God, you know how much I've tried to talk her into a better life... a productive life... a life of purpose and fulfillment. Lord, you know how I have prayed for her... for 20 long years I have prayed for her... prayed for her to be able to give up her drug addiction... but she hasn't done it, Lord. She hasn't made the right decisions.

And now, here we are... waiting to find out what and why the court decided what they did. This judge seems to have been involved with her for a long time. I will hear something soon... and then the phone rings.

The young talented prosecutor did her job well. She stands and talks about my daughter for over 30 minutes. She is prepared... very well prepared. She has a very thick file on Lori... all her attempts in rehab... all her outpatient therapy is documented. All of the times she walked out on the help provided for her is also there in her thick file... all the dirty drug tests... all the times that she didn't show up for her probation appointments... all the times that she just shrugged off her community service sentences... all the times that she walked out of halfway house therapy... all of it... all of it... It's all there... all there in the very thick file. This all goes back to high school days... the trouble... the fights... the traffic violations... the addiction... it all goes back so far...

And it's all there... in black and white... written down in her big file...

And she reads it all... declares it all for the court to hear it.   She has started her presentation with the letter that Lori has written to the court... asking for another chance... another opportunity to get clean... another stay in the halfway house. However, there is also another letter in the file... from the halfway house. They no longer will take her back. She has burned her bridges with them. She has run away from there more than once... disrespected their program. Why would another chance be any different than the ones she has already had?   They will not take her back. The halfway house is done with Lori.

Then there's the drug court program that she was placed in about a year ago. Surely this will work. She can live in the YWCA ... she can go to drug court...check in everyday....go to outpatient therapy... get a part time job... stay out of jail this way. Surely this will work for Lori. Now she tells the court that this would be a good thing to try again... even though she walked out on that program a few months back and didn't complete it... and of course, continued to produce dirty drug tests.   But there is a problem... there's another letter in the file. This one is from the drug court program. They have decided not to take her back into that program. She has burned her bridges with them, too.   No more chances for her there... They are done with her. They don't feel that they can help her. Drug court is no longer an option, declares the determined prosecutor. The judge listens patiently... listens to all that is said... listens to the content of the file.

So does Lori. She stands there in her jailhouse outfit... that orange scrub suit... dressed like all the other inmates. This is the girl who has always loved cute clothes... who has had so many clothes... who has given them away to friends so freely... because she had so many. She used to love to look good... to be stunning... charming... and oh, so pretty. She used to want to make the men's heads turn... yes, she used to really care about all of that. Now, she will wear look alike scrubs for a very long time. No more cute dresses... great shoes... no more of all of that for now... She stands there... waiting... waiting on the judge to speak. And then he does.

He is compassionate, it seems. He is older. He has seen so many come through his court room just like Lori... He has seen them, he says. He has often given them several chances to change... often put them on house arrest... but they can still get drugs, can't they?

Lori has so much going for her... or at least it appears that she could have, if she truly changed. He is going to help her... the only way he can... he is going to take a firm stand... he doesn't want her to overdose on drugs... as have other young people like her. He tells of others that ended up dead... actually dead from their ugly habit... dead... no more chances... they were gone. That was it. He doesn't want that to happen to Lori... He wants her to live. He really does.

He has decided to help her live... the only way he knows how. She will have a five year prison sentence. She will serve at least two years of that... it depends on her... her behavior... how soon she will be released. It depends on what she does with this new chance he is giving her. He is giving her an opportunity to live... and to change... It is now up to her... up to Lori... this beautiful drug addicted young woman... this mother of a young son... yes, this woman standing before him is being given an opportunity to live and not die. This is her chance to change. Will she take this open door and make the changes necessary to live? This is her decision. She is now led from the courtroom... out the door... back to her jail cell... to begin the next phase of her life. The future has just begun...

Marcia McAllister

CHAPTER TWO
Voices and Choices

May 2, 2010

Well, daughter... this has been a very hard week! I know it has for you... but it also has for me. I knew this was probably coming down for you... sentencing to prison... but to hear the words that it has happened... was totally overwhelming for me. Even as I write this, my heart is aching for you... I can't stop the tears... I want to hold my little girl... and make it all better... take it all away... and give you a fresh new hope and new start. And even as I write this, I realize that I cannot do that for you... these are choices you have made... this is a way of life that you kept choosing for so many years. HOWEVER... here's the good news... you don't have to continue on this same old drug addicted, lying, stealing, deceiving way of life that you have been on... IT CAN CHANGE NOW... You can finally realize that all of that... has gotten you right where you are.

Lori, you know that I have always told you and your brothers that you can be anything you put your mind to be... you can become all that God has planned for you... or you can become all that the devil has planned for you... Because that is really what it's ultimately all about... God vs. the devil... Good vs. evil... Becoming all that God has planned for you... vs... falling into all the traps and schemes of the devil to destroy you. Remember what Jesus said in John 10:10...

"THE THIEF COMES TO STEAL, KILL AND DESTROY... BUT I HAVE COME TO GIVE YOU LIFE... LIFE ABUNDANTLY..."

Those are His words... words to give you hope... words to bless you when you are discouraged... words to help you sort out all the decisions you have made for so many years... The devil has had you right where he wanted you! I know this is true... because I know that God has had a call on your life since you were born... but the rebellion in you said... "No way... I'm going to do my own thing... I'm going to run from my calling... not run to it... I'm going to party... beat the system... stay drugged up... I'll avoid ever having to really face my issues... I'm going to do what I want... when I want... and no one can stop me!" That's the lie of the devil... and you have lived that way... far too long... But, God did stop you... and there you are... in a situation where you will have to stop and listen... listen to God...

And you are now clean and sober... so you will hear His voice clearly, won't you? He is speaking to you... probably right now as you read this letter from your Mama... who loves you so much and wants only the best for you... yes, probably now you will listen... all the voices and choices that the devil has placed in your head all these years... all of that... must bow it's knee to the name of Jesus... which I speak over you right now as I write this... that name that is above every name... that name that is above rebellion... above drug addiction... that name that can set the captive free... you, my daughter... the captive for so many years... yes, you... Now is the time for you to sit back and look at your life... all of it... all the disappointments... all the mistakes... all the wrong decisions... and do something about it... It starts with you asking God to forgive you... then it moves on to you forgiving yourself... starting over... You make a quality decision to start over... Look at these words in Psalm 32, in the Message Bible...written by David... so long ago...

"COUNT YOURSELF LUCKY, HOW HAPPY YOU MUST BE... YOU GET A FRESH START, YOUR SLATE'S WIPED CLEAN.

COUNT YOURSELF LUCKY. GOD HOLDS NOTHING AGAINST YOU AND YOU'RE HOLDING NOTHING BACK FROM HIM.

WHEN I KEPT IT ALL INSIDE, MY BONES TURNED TO POWDER, MY WORDS BECAME DAYLONG GROANS.

THE PRESSURE NEVER LET UP; ALL THE JUICES OF MY LIFE DRIED UP.

THEN I LET IT ALL OUT; I SAID, "I'LL MAKE A CLEAN BREAST OF MY FAILURES TO GOD." SUDDENLY THE PRESSURE WAS GONE... MY GUILT DISSOLVED, MY SIN DISAPPEARD.

I love you so much... and yes, this too shall pass... but this time... this time... let this be the BIG LESSON of your life... come out of there a brand new woman... and while you're there... be the minister and missionary that God has called you to be... this is just a new mission field... are you called of God to serve there? Only you can answer that...

I love you so much... God showed me this morning as I was praying for you, the day in Stuart, Florida at the church Grandpa was pastoring... when you, your Dad, Ryan and I stood up front with Aunt Karen, Uncle Terry and Eric and Jenny....and how Grandpa prayed over you... you and Eric were 3-4 month old babies... and how we dedicated you to God... God showed me this morning... that I gave you to God... I have so wanted to always take you back... make you understand what you need to understand... pound some sense into you... all of it to make you see the error of your ways... but I can't... it's all up to God...

and He loves you so very much... as do all of us... your whole family... We all love you... and we want you to turn this all around for your good!

I know you can do this, Lori... you can become the woman that God created you to be... it starts right now... with your decisions... your attitudes... your desires... run to God, daughter... He is your hope, your strength, your joy... He will renew your strength... you will get through all of this... and you will come out strong... strong in God... and already on the path God has set for you... that's my prayer for you...

Be encouraged this day... the drugs, the lifestyle... could have killed you... could have turned your brain to mush... but it didn't happen... God has preserved you... your best friend, Marcy didn't make it... she died... but you are going to make it, Lori... God has a plan for you... now, figure it all out... FORGIVE, FORGIVE, FORGIVE... and get started really living...

I love you, my daughter...

YOUR MOM... who birthed you and loves you so very much... and always will.

CHAPTER THREE
In The Beginning

January 21, 1976

Dear daughter,

It was really cold and snowy on January 20, 1976. Your Dad was an emergency room doctor... and on a 24 hour shift at the hospital when I began to go into labor. Your two year old brother, Ryan was asleep in his comfy bed... not knowing that he would soon see his little baby sister. Actually, he thought you were going to be a baby brother... as did your Dad and I. Those were the days before ultrasound... somehow we just thought you were going to be a boy. I think we thought that based on your heart beat rate. Anyway, there I was sitting on the sofa in our beautiful home... watching some TV... trying to relax... with such a huge belly and pains beginning to course through my body.

Your Dad kept calling... "what was I feeling...? Did I want him to come on home... get another doctor to take his place?" "No", I said... "I'm ok right now." My parents lived in Florida. Except for friends... I was alone. As the evening progressed, I knew I needed to go to the hospital. It was over an hour and a half away... in Indianapolis. I called your Dad... "you better get your Dad to come on down to the house and stay with Ryan", I said... "I'm feeling much worse." It was snowing harder now... Soon your Grandpa called... he was on his way... By the time he arrived, I had a little bag packed... and was ready. Your Dad and Grandpa arrived about the same time. We got in the car... hugged Grandpa and baby Ryan good-bye and headed out in the snow storm.

As we got closer and closer to Indianapolis... my pains left ... they were suddenly gone.

Your Dad, being the wise doctor that he was, decided that we were not turning around and going back home. We would go on to Indianapolis and get a hotel room and wait on you for awhile. We checked into a beautiful hotel... close to the hospital. The people at the front desk remarked on my huge tummy... full of baby. We told them that my pains had stopped and we were going to try to get some rest. They told us our room was on them... for as long as we needed it. That was cool... so up to our room we went.

I remember your tired Daddy climbing into bed and falling asleep quickly. I also remember your expectant Mommy, me... trying to lie down... couldn't get comfortable... sat up... started to walk around the room and began to have those wonderful contractions again. This went on for quite some time... or so it seemed. Actually, from the time we checked in... until the time we checked out was only a couple of hours. So off to the hospital we went. The dreaded long hours of labor began. You were finally on the way.

I had called my parents... your Grandma and Grandpa... in Florida, of course... and Grandma had planned on coming up to Indiana to stay with us for a couple of weeks after you were born. She got on a plane that morning... Jan. 21 and made her way up to the airport at Indianapolis. She called the hospital and talked to your Dad who told her to get a taxi and come to the hospital. You were almost ready to be born... and then, there you were!!

But wait a minute... we thought you were going to be a boy. The doctor and your Dad began to say... oh, my... this is a surprise... and then they laid you in my arms... my beautiful little daughter... there you were... Christy Lynn... my daughter. Well, that is what we named you... that day...

The next day your Dad came back to the hospital to tell me that your brother Ryan was having such a hard time with your name that he thought we should change it.   He and Ryan had decided to name you Lori Lynn.   Lynn... after your Aunt Karen, my sister... and her daughter, Jennifer Lynn.   That was fine with me... so your name was changed.

Now, that brings me to an interesting aspect of your little personality as a child.   You were always changing your name. When you were about 2 or 2½... in the nursery at church... you told the workers that you had changed your name.   When I went to pick you up after church one Sunday, the lady working the nursery that day said they had all been laughing at you so much.   You told them all not to call you Lori anymore.   Your new name was JELLO JONES... and so you became Jello Jones... to so many at our church. Where you got that, I have no idea.

When you were about 3½, you were playing on our family room floor with your baby brother, Marc... and you said... "Mommy, we have new names now. Marc is now Marcus Bubilas and I am Charla Hella Bubilas...!!!!!" Wow... where did all that come from? It must be your wonderful, silly personality that God gave you... your fun loving, crazy, entertaining self... that God created you to be.   Which, of course, brings me to this point... the point of this letter to you, my daughter, you are gifted... you are full of charm and wit... and so much fun to be around... Yes, that is you. You have that silly sense of humor that I love so much. I love to laugh with you... tell you some of my crazy real estate stories and watch you crack up in laughter.   We see so much of life the same. So many things that make you laugh about situations in which you find yourself... make me laugh, too. Your sense of humor also reminds me of the good times with your Dad. You're a lot like him, too... and that's a good thing.

I'm reminded of this Scripture right now as I write this. These also are words of David... found in Psalm 139: 13-16

"OH YES, YOU SHAPED ME FIRST INSIDE, THEN OUT; YOU FORMED ME IN MY MOTHER'S WOMB. I THANK YOU, HIGH GOD --- YOU'RE BREATHTAKING!

BODY AND SOUL, I AM MARVELOUSLY MADE! I WORSHIP IN ADORATION---WHAT A CREATION! YOU KNOW ME INSIDE AND OUT, YOU KNOW EVERY BONE IN MY BODY;

YOU KNOW EXACTLY HOW I WAS MADE, BIT BY BIT, HOW I WAS SCULPTED FROM NOTHING INTO SOMETHING.
LIKE AN OPEN BOOK, YOU WATCHED ME GROW FROM CONCEPTION TO BIRTH;
ALL THE STAGES OF MY LIFE WERE SPREAD OUT BEFORE YOU.

THE DAYS OF MY LIFE ALL PREPARED BEFORE I'D EVEN LIVED ONE DAY."

And so you see, daughter,   God knows everything there is to know about you.

He made you... and as much as your Dad and I and your brothers and family love you... God loves you so much more!!   He made you... He knows you inside and out. There is nothing hidden from Him. All your desires, all that is you, Lori... He knows... All that makes you who you are... He created... and He knows you... all you feel... all you've done... all of it!!

Now, here's the really cool part... HE LOVES YOU... IN SPITE OF ANYTHING AND EVERYTHING YOU'VE EVER DONE... All the mistakes... all the sin... all the rebellion... all the lying, stealing, drugging, all of it... HE LOVES YOU THROUGH IT ALL... and He always will! There is nothing you can do to keep Him from loving you.
David also said in Psalm 103: 3-6

"HE FORGIVES YOUR SINS—EVERY ONE.
HE HEALS YOUR DISEASES—EVERY ONE.

HE REDEEMS YOU FROM HELL—SAVES YOUR LIFE!   HE CROWNS YOU WITH LOVE AND MERCY—A PARADISE CROWN.

HE WRAPS YOU IN GOODNESS—BEAUTY ETERNAL.   HE RENEWS YOUR YOUTH — YOU'RE ALWAYS YOUNG IN HIS PRESENCE.

GOD MAKES EVERYTHING COME OUT RIGHT; HE PUTS VICTIMS BACK ON THEIR FEET... GOD IS SHEER MERCY AND GRACE; NOT EASILY ANGERED, HE'S RICH IN LOVE.

HE DOESN'T TREAT US AS OUR SINS DESERVE, NOR PAY US BACK IN FULL FOR OUR WRONGS. AS HIGH AS HEAVEN IS OVER THE EARTH, SO STRONG IS HIS LOVE TO THOSE WHO FEAR HIM.

AND AS FAR AS SUNRISE IS FROM SUNSET, HE HAS SEPARATED US FROM OUR SINS.   AS PARENTS FEEL FOR THEIR CHILDREN, GOD FEELS FOR THOSE WHO FEAR HIM. HE KNOWS US INSIDE AND OUT, KEEPS IN MIND THAT WE'RE MADE OF MUD."

Wow... doesn't that help you? Remember that God's Word is alive... and able to get down on the inside of us... and change our thinking. I pray right now that these words will do just that for you, Lori. Study these words... read them over and over... get them down on the inside of you... memorize them... Let these words change you.

And so, dear daughter... you are not just my daughter... or your Dad's... you are most importantly... God's daughter.

Look at Isaiah 43:2

"DON'T BE AFRAID, I'VE REDEEMED YOU. I'VE CALLED YOUR NAME. YOU'RE MINE. WHEN YOU'RE IN OVER YOUR HEAD, I'LL BE WITH YOU. WHEN YOU'RE IN ROUGH WATERS, YOU WILL NOT GO DOWN, WHEN YOU'RE BETWEEN A ROCK AND A HARD PLACE, IT WON'T BE A DEAD END-- BECAUSE I AM GOD, YOUR PERSONAL GOD, THE HOLY ONE OF ISRAEL, YOUR SAVIOR. I PAID A HUGE PRICE FOR YOU... THAT'S HOW MUCH I LOVE YOU! I'D SELL OFF THE WHOLE WORLD TO GET YOU BACK, TRADE THE CREATION JUST FOR YOU."

I love those words... Let them speak to you... speak to your identity... you are HIS, daughter... you are GOD's child... not just mine... but, especially HIS. You can't run from that anymore... because anywhere you have run... He has always been there... waiting on you... seeing you through each situation... protecting you... keeping you alive... FOR SUCH A TIME AS THIS... your moment of decision... your time to CHANGE and turn your life around...

All for Him... all for His glory...

I love you... and am praying for you... even as I am writing these words... YOUR MOM

CHAPTER FOUR
It's Time To See Clearly

Dear daughter,

Well, it appears that these letters are becoming a new book... a book dedicated to you... a book all about you... but also, a book, I hope, that will help other families who have been so affected by the horrors of drug addiction. I know that there are so many families like us out there, Lori. They are there... struggling with all the problems that come with this awful addiction... all the craziness... all the anger, all the disappointment and hurt. This is common... all of this. I know this and I pray that as I write to you... many, many people will be blessed by our story. It is OUR story... not just yours... all of your family and friends... and especially your precious little son, Levi... are affected... It's all our story... we're in this together!

Our story, Lori... is all about so many factors. It's not one thing that brought all this on you... it's so many aspects of your life that all came together to allow you to become so addicted to drugs.

Today I'm reminded of your eyes. It wasn't until you were almost four years old that we began to notice that there was something wrong with your eyesight. As you played with your brothers, different situations began to happen that showed us that you couldn't really see very well. I remember taking you to the eye doctor and listening to him as he explained how very bad your eyes were. I was surprised... and actually upset with myself that we hadn't noticed this earlier. I remember when you did get your little "coke bottle" glasses... so thick... because your eyes were so bad... that you actually told me... "Mommy, there's only one Marky"...your little brother... you seemed to have been seeing two of him... and we didn't even know that.

You were seeing life very differently than your brothers, your Dad or I, were. Now, I wonder if you haven't always seen life from a very different perspective. Having such bad eyes caused you to feel bad about yourself... you were teased at school... you were called names... you were bothered by how you looked. Of course, we thought you were so cute in your little glasses with the rainbow insignia on the right glass... that you picked out... but you didn't think you were cute. You would cry about how you looked and how you felt. I hated it that you were hurting and always tried to reassure you that you were so beautiful and so special... which you are!

However, I now know that the devil began to harass you at an early age... to attempt to destroy your self esteem... to really get you down on yourself... to take away all your self confidence. Again, as I write this... very early one Tuesday morning, I am sitting here at my desk with the tears just flowing down. You know, as a mother, how much you hurt when your child is hurting. It just tears you up, as a parent. You want to change the situation for your child. You want to take away the pain, the suffering. I am feeling this right now... I am feeling what I felt so many years ago when you would cry about your glasses and how you were teased. I am allowing God to soothe me with His precious comfort as I write these words.

I could not change any of that back then... only hold you and tell you it would all be fine... that you were indeed beautiful and talented and smart. All of which was... and still is... very true. But somehow Lori... the devil got in there. He saw a "crack in your armor" so to speak and began to chip away at your feelings of inferiority and insecurity. He began to magnify those feelings and tell you that you were "LESS THAN"... less than your brothers... less than your friends without glasses... all of it. Those feelings went deep inside. You see, daughter, the devil works by the POWER OF SUGGESTION...

Jesus said in John 8 that the devil is a liar and the father of lies. Yes, that's what he does. That's his M.O. (modus operandi)... that's how he works. He suggests to us something like this... that you are not as cute, smart, attractive... all of it... as others without poor eyesight... then you begin to "buy the lie"... you think... that's true... that's how I'm feeling... so that must be true... and so the lie becomes part of your truth... ever so cleverly... the lie becomes truth to you... not truth to others... just truth to you... The very sad part of this is that if this is not caught quickly and the lie destroyed, it continues to grow within you and bring on other issues with it. I think I'll tell you about some of those in later letters. For now, let's talk about this inferiority, insecurity and unworthiness... the 3 enemies... not the 3 amigos... the 3 enemies. They are strong as they unite to destroy you. The Lord has been showing me this for you for some time now. I know there is a solution to this... found in God's Word... so here goes... listen up, daughter and LIVE!!

First, we must establish that the Word is our final authority on all that concerns us. Some might dispute that... but I have lived it all my life. I know it's true... and you know the Word is TRUTH. People can debate certain topics... but God's Word changes us. I have seen so many miracles... and you have too, by the way... as people began to line up their thoughts and emotions with the LIVING WORD of GOD.

II Timothy 3:14-17 says this in the Message Bible:

"BUT DON'T LET IT FAZE YOU. STICK WITH WHAT YOU LEARNED AND BELIEVED, SURE OF THE INTEGRITY OF YOUR TEACHERS—WHY, YOU TOOK IN THE SACRED SCRIPTURES WITH YOUR MOTHER'S MILK! THERE'S NOTHING LIKE THE WRITTEN WORD OF GOD FOR SHOWING YOU THE WAY TO SALVATION THROUGH FAITH IN CHRIST JESUS. EVERY PART OF SCRIPTURE IS GOD-BREATHED AND USEFUL ONE WAY OR ANOTHER—SHOWING US TRUTH, EXPOSING OUR REBELLION, CORRECT-ING OUR MISTAKES, TRAINING US TO LIVE GOD'S WAY. THROUGH THE WORD WE ARE PUT TOGETHER AND SHAPED UP FOR THE TASKS GOD HAS FOR US."

And yes, Lori from the time you were born... you were around the Word... in the Word... learning the Word at the Christian school you attended for your first few years. You heard the Word... actually you have always loved God's Word. In so many times that God has spoken to your heart in a service... while I was preaching the Word... I have seen your eyes well up with tears as God spoke to you. I have seen you make your way to the altar for prayer. I have held you in my arms as you cried out to God to make you strong against this addiction. I've seen all that several times, haven't I?

Some would say... well, it didn't work... all that prayer for her. Oh yes, it has. The prayers of your family and friends have protected you... have brought you to this place of huge decision... this place of quietness before God... no more running, partying and playing. It's time to make quality decisions that will shape your life and the life of your young son forever.

A few days ago I watched the actor, Michael Douglas, being interviewed on the Today Show. His son, Cameron, has just been sentenced to five years in prison... just like you. Michael said that this had to happen because if not... Cameron would have killed himself with drugs... or been killed by someone else... that now he has a chance to live and have a fresh start. I, of course, thought of you. Yes, this is your fresh start... your God given opportunity to become all that God has ordained you to be... To think straight... to make the right decisions... to become so strong on the inside... that no lie of the devil can, in any way influence you to go back again to the life of drugs and all it brings with it.

Isaiah 45: 22-23: "SO TURN TO ME AND BE HELPED-SAVED! EVERYONE, WHOEVER AND WHEREVER YOU ARE. I AM GOD, THE ONLY GOD THERE IS, THE ONE AND ONLY. I PROMISE IN MY OWN NAME; EVERY WORD OUT OF MY MOUTH DOES WHAT IT SAYS. I NEVER TAKE BACK WHAT I SAY"

Those are God's words to you... turn to Him and be helped... His Word is true to you. Look at these words in Isaiah 43: 18-21:

"FORGET ABOUT WHAT'S HAPPENED; DON'T KEEP GOING OVER OLD HISTORY.

BE ALERT, BE PRESENT. I'M ABOUT TO DO SOMETHING BRAND-NEW. IT'S BURSTING OUT! DON'T YOU SEE IT? THERE IT IS! I'M MAKING A ROAD THROUGH THE DESERT, RIVERS IN THE BADLANDS... DRINKING WATER FOR THE PEOPLE I CHOSE, THE PEOPLE I MADE ESPECIALLY FOR MYSELF, A PEOPLE CUSTOM-MADE TO PRAISE ME."

Yes, Lori... that's you... You are created to be to the praise of His glory... and you can be just that. You can be such a testimony of God's great power... of His ability to change a life... of His ability to change desires and cravings. You can be that one that is totally set free from all the years of addictions and bad decisions. Your mind can be so renewed... so changed... that you don't think the same anymore. No more of all those years of trying to kill the pain of your emotions by drugging yourself up... so you don't feel. You need to feel it... just as I am feeling all of this as I am writing to you. I had to move my box of Kleenex to my desk as the tears flow from my eyes and heart for you. You need to feel it... and face it... and then forgive ... forgive yourself and all those around you who may knowingly or unknowingly have contributed to your addiction.

Forgiveness does not mean that we agree with what was said or done. It just means that the person... even ourselves... cannot change it or make it right... they don't owe us anymore... we cancel the debt that they owe us... we let it go... once and for all. Yes, I'm sure there are so many to forgive... including your family... but you can do all this... with the help of God's Holy Spirit showing you who to forgive. Don't be surprised if you wake up in the middle of the night seeing a situation that happened to you... maybe a long time ago... you might almost relive it in your mind and heart. When that happens, that's the Holy Spirit bringing a situation to your consciousness that you need to deal with... that you need to forgive. Do it quickly... let it all go... allow yourself to feel the emotions of that moment... and then, by an act of your will... decide to forgive... to let it go... they don't owe you anymore... they can't make it right... Destroy the power of that incident by forgiveness... It actually loses all power over you... as you forgive!!

And then, by an act of your will... fall out of agreement with those old thought patterns... decide to think about that person or situation the way God would... just release them to God... let Him do the work in them that needs to be done. That burden is not for you to bear. Let it go... You remember in AA they always say... "LET GO AND LET GOD!" ... Well, that's it... Let Go and Let God!

And so, my daughter, I take the God given authority that I have in the name of Jesus and I pray for you this day... that you would refuse those feelings of inferiority, insecurity and unworthiness... for you are worthy... worthy to become whole in God... worthy to be truly emotionally healed... from the inside out... worthy to receive all the blessings of God that He has for you... worthy to see yourself and others... but especially yourself... with new eyes... the eyes of God... and see just how very special you are... how blessed to be alive... how blessed to be a mother of a beautiful son... how blessed to be given another opportunity to get it all right this time... to become totally and completely set free from your addictions... yes, you are blessed... LOOK AT YOURSELF THAT WAY... DAUGHTER... through the eyes of forgiveness and blessing.

It is all there for you... just walk through that open door into your new day... your day of forgiveness and emotional healing!

I love you so much... I see you out of there someday... a brand new creation of God... I see you ministering to others that God can also set them free... I see you feeling confident that you are God's precious child... that all is forgiven... that this is a new day... I see you healed!

So much love to you this day...
from YOUR MOM...
who is always here for you!

CHAPTER FIVE

Maybe So. . . Maybe Not!

Dear daughter,

I hope you know just how very much you are on my heart and my mind. I wake up wondering how you are... what your life is really like in that place of confinement. I wonder how you are adjusting... are you scared? Are you beginning to process yet... all that you need to work through? I know that it has been a few months now since you've been able to get drugs and alcohol. Surely your mind must be much clearer than it's been for so many years.

Lori, my mind goes to you as a young five year old. I certainly remember how very cute you were... how silly... how much fun you always enjoyed with your neighbor friends...especially Kelly. You two were great friends. I see you now as that five year old and remember your very strong will. Actually, I have always said that you were the hardest one of my

33

three children to discipline. When you put your mind to something... you were very hard to convince otherwise. When you decided that you weren't going to behave... or that you were going to do something your way... well, it was so hard to change your decision... even if it was good for you.

I guess some people would call you... the STRONG WILLED CHILD. I think that term has been around for awhile. "Strong willed" is probably a good description of you. I might also add words like... "stubborn" and "has to get her own way." Yes, daughter, that is you... always determined to do "it" your way... regardless of the opinions of your parents or even teachers, in some instances.

Shortly after I opened the Christian bookstore with a friend, I remember an incident very clearly that happened with you. I was only working part time and your Dad was taking a morning off from work and was taking care of you and your brothers. About mid morning you all showed up at the bookstore very upset. Your Dad had tried very hard to get you to take your vitamin that morning. As I remember we had been having a very difficult time with you on this issue. That particular morning he had decided to push the issue... since, of course, he was a doctor and knew you needed to take that vitamin. You said "NO". He said "YES" and so the struggle began. He described the incident very clearly. I understood... as I also had those kinds of scenes with you over your vitamins.

Evidently you had lied to him about taking the pill because he had followed you as you stormed to your room and he watched you put something under your dresser. He gave you every opportunity to tell the truth... to tell what you were doing. Now remember... you were only five years old. As usual, a showdown ensued and you stuck to your story... There was nothing, supposedly, under the dresser. But there was... wasn't there? When you refused repeatedly to reveal the truth about the vitamin, he pulled the dresser out and saw for himself the whole truth. There it was. Not only was the vitamin in question there... but many others were also stashed there. How surprised and disappointed he was! He loaded you all up and brought you to the bookstore for a family meeting. He wanted help getting you to realize that you cannot lie and deceive like that. We talked to you about the seriousness of this... but what really happened that day, Lori? Did anything change within you in regard to lying and deceiving?

One of the things that a lot of people pride themselves in... is their word... telling the truth... standing by their convictions. But all of that seems to have been foreign to you from an early age. I can honestly say that you have only gotten worse in this area as you have grown up. How many times have you heard me say, "LORI, THE CONSISTENT THING ABOUT YOU IS YOUR INCONSISTENCY?" Without totally be-laboring this point, I can say that you have lived your life... up till now, with little or no consistency. It seems that the addictions have only made this worse. In order to live the lifestyle you have lived... lying, stealing, deceiving have become a way of life for you. It's all there... all of it. You have lived this way for so long... always trying to cover up a situation or action... by lying... by deceiving... by not following through on your commitments... by living very inconsistently. This has been such a problem that I know you cannot possibly name all the places you have ever lived... or all the people you have lived with. It would be impossible for you to do so. Just your living conditions alone have changed sometimes 10-12 times a year... or even more in some years. All of that is hard for me to understand. It speaks one word to me... CHAOS!

The older I get and the more that I teach the Word, I find that some aspects of life become simpler. Now that might sound confusing but it's really not. I said to you in another letter recently that life is a battle between good and evil... between doing your own thing... vs. doing what God wants you to do. Actually, I said that it can boil down to a battle between what the devil wants for you and what God has planned for you. I really do believe that.

I also know that the devil is a master in the area of CHAOS. He is so good at it that often we fail to recognize his hand in our lives in this area. We get caught up in the "drama" of the moment... what this person did or said... and how wrong it was... or how you were treated at work, etc... Drama, drama, drama... Hasn't drama been a huge part of your life?

I know the answer... it is a resounding YES! The devil loves drama because it often causes such chaos that our attention is drawn to the event or the person we are upset with! We are almost blinded to the fact that the devil has engineered yet another chaotic situation so that we can remain busy telling all our friends the latest injustice. This chaos also gives people plenty of justification for using drugs or alcohol. The substance numbs their thinking... they no longer even want to work out a situation, but often love to just rehash all the wrongs and hurts. Does any of this remind you of situations you have lived? I know the answer... yes, it does.

Lori, it's all about the battle between CHAOS and PEACE in our lives! It's really very simple. The devil wants you always inconsistent... always on the move... always upset about something or someone. God, on the other hand, is the God of PEACE! Remember in Luke 2 when the shepherds were out taking care of their sheep and suddenly God's angel was standing there with all the bright light?

The angel was joined by a huge angelic choir singing praises to God... announcing the birth of Jesus. They sang, "GLORY TO GOD IN THE HEAVENLY HEIGHTS. PEACE TO ALL MEN AND WOMEN ON EARTH WHO PLEASE HIM."

What did the angels say God was bringing through the birth of His son? Yes, there it is... PEACE! ...

Also, in Isaiah 9:6... written some 700-800 years before Jesus was born, it was prophesied...

"FOR A CHILD WILL BE BORN TO US, A SON WILL BE GIVEN TO US; AND THE GOVERNMENT WILL REST ON HIS SHOULDERS; AND HIS NAME WILL BE CALLED WONDERFUL COUNSELOR, MIGHTY GOD, ETERNAL FATHER, PRINCE OF PEACE."

Yes, there it is again... Jesus is the Prince of Peace. He came to bring Peace... to teach us how to live in peace... not chaos. I love this verse because it also says that He is our Wonderful Counselor. Amen. He's the best counselor... the Holy Spirit within us is the very best counselor! He can get through to us when no one else can. He can bring the peace you so need... teach you how to live in peace and take away the craving for chaos. He not only can do this... but He wants to do it for you!

In John 14:27... before Jesus went back up to heaven... after the resurrection, he said this:

"I'M TELLING YOU THESE THINGS WHILE I'M STILL LIVING WITH YOU. THE FRIEND, THE HOLY SPIRIT WHOM THE FATHER WILL SEND AT MY REQUEST, WILL MAKE EVERYTHING PLAIN TO YOU. HE WILL REMIND YOU OF ALL THE THINGS I HAVE TOLD YOU. I'M LEAVING YOU WELL AND WHOLE. THAT'S MY PARTING GIFT TO YOU. PEACE. I DON'T LEAVE YOU THE

WAY YOU'RE USED TO BEING LEFT---FEELING ABANDONED, BEREFT. SO DON'T BE UPSET. DON'T BE DISTRAUGHT."

Jesus came to bring peace to our troubled lives. Paul said in Romans 5:1 in the NASB translation,

"THEREFORE HAVING BEEN JUSTIFIED BY FAITH, WE HAVE PEACE WITH GOD THROUGH OUR LORD JESUS CHRIST." In the Message Bible,

Romans 5:1-2 says this: "BY ENTERING THROUGH FAITH INTO WHAT GOD HAS ALWAYS WANTED TO DO FOR US—SET US RIGHT WITH HIM, MAKE US FIT FOR HIM—WE HAVE IT ALL TOGETHER WITH GOD BECAUSE OF OUR MASTER JESUS. AND THAT'S NOT ALL: WE THROW OPEN OUR DOORS TO GOD AND DISCOVER AT THE SAME MOMENT THAT HE HAS ALREADY THROWN OPEN HIS DOOR TO US. WE FIND OURSELVES STANDING WHERE WE ALWAYS HOPED WE MIGHT STAND—OUT IN THE WIDE OPEN SPACES OF GOD'S GRACE AND GLORY, STANDING TALL AND SHOUTING OUR PRAISE."

And that is exactly where I see you, my daughter... standing in the wide open spaces of God's grace and glory. One of these days, you will be out of prison ... out of the confinement. Actually, you've been in that place of restriction and confinement most of your life... because of your choices... your craving for chaos... for the drugs that would numb you and keep you from facing what you needed to face in your life. But this is a new day for you... a day to start living now in the wide open spaces of God's grace. Remember grace is best defined as God's unmerited favor... when we don't deserve His favor... we have it anyway... because of His great love for us.

So there you have it... your new choices can be for truth, consistency, peace, grace... all of it... instead of all that your life has been. I know you can make the right choices, Lori. You have a strong will and you can make good choices. You can live the rest of your life drug free and pursuing PEACE! Yes you can!

Through many years of being around people who have struggled with addiction, I have noticed that most of these never take the time necessary to really "stop the merry-go-round" and get off the ride. A few days in jail, here and there, doesn't do the work necessary to change the craving for the chaos... instead, it seems to only make them more anxious to get out and live the way they want to live. I know the jail system is meant to deter the offender, but from watching so many... and watching you all these years... I really don't think a few days in jail does a whole lot for most drug abusers. I know that when you were in jail here in Florida for those ten days after those drug violations you seemed determined to come out of there and "do better". I really don't remember much change at all, however. Now, looking back, I think that your determination to "do better" was half-hearted at best. Nothing had really changed in you. Yes, you were uncomfortable in jail and you absolutely hated the days in maximum security... but nothing really changed after you got out of jail. I remember you describing how you felt during that jail stay, but obviously those feelings weren't strong enough to bring about the total change that you needed... then, and that you need now.

I really believe that to be finally free of drug and alcohol abuse will require a spiritual change within you. That's why I am writing certain Scriptures to you that I know are sent to help you make the changes necessary. The whole AA program is based on a spiritual awakening, isn't it? That's the answer, Lori... and that's precisely why I believe that you can change "for good" this time... that this whole prison sentence is going to be used by God to give you plenty of time to do the work within yourself that is so needed... so that this will genuinely be the big crossroads experience in your life. This is it. This is your opportunity to really face your attitudes, decisions and actions that have contributed to the using all these years. And yes, daughter, I do believe that you can turn all this around for your good. You can become all that God has planned for you. You can really, really change this time... and it will last. This is your MOMENT OF DECISION... YOUR OPPORTUNITY FOR A FRESH START!

This is it! Make the most of it!

I love and miss you so much... and pray for you that you take all these words very seriously... your life... and the peace of your precious son, Levi... depend on it!

YOUR MOM

ADDENDUM
Referencing Chapters 1-5

May 5, 2010.

I must add a section right now to this manuscript. First of all, this work has obviously been in the making since 1976, when Lori was brought into this world. At the time that she was born, her Dad and I had no clue, of course, of all the many challenges that would present themselves to us as this precious child began to grow and live with us. She seemed to be unique in so many ways. She was our only daughter, born between two sons. She was always the child that presented all the interesting situations or challenges, if you will. She was the one that seemed "different" in so many ways, from her brothers. To this day, her brothers are alike in many ways. They are honest, sweet and full of integrity. They are both very successful in their professions and love the Lord with all their hearts. They both are allowing God to use them in so many ways. I am very proud of them and all that they have accomplished.

But now, back to Lori. I did not intend to write a book about my daughter. I can honestly say that the Holy Spirit has prompted this project... put it deep within my heart and given me the desire and compulsion to get this story out for others to learn from our experience with a drug addicted daughter. Also, I am finding that as I write these words... I, myself, am receiving healing from God... finding comfort from Him as I remember these incidents in Lori's life. Actually, it's absolutely amazing to be experiencing all of this as I write. I do not have a master outline of what I want to present. I am allowing God's Holy Spirit to direct each chapter... as I write to her. As I write these words, I do not know what Chapter six is going to be about. But I do know that God knows already. He has it all planned out. He also knows the people... the families... that need this book. There are so many of you out there that are struggling with the same issues that we have fought, for over twenty years now.

And so, for you... I pray that your eyes will be opened to the truths that you need to see as you read. Perhaps you will even cry a few tears as you relate to incidents or attitudes that you have seen in someone close to you that suffers from these same addictions. I pray that God will minister to you, as you read... I pray that He will give you new hope, new desire to become closer to Him and find your strength and joy in Him. He really is the answer to all of this. He has allowed me to find that real and deep peace in Him as I have been working through all of this... her current prison sentence and all that it entails.

I also have found, as I write, that the Holy Spirit is showing me metaphors in her life that I have never seen or even thought of before. I want to share with you some of those that I am now seeing... as they come to mind.

First of all, Lori's eyes....She never could see clearly physically... and still can't... emotionally and spiritually she has never really seen clearly. She seems to be looking through glasses that are all distorted. Her priorities, her desires... all of it have been greatly "out of whack"... so to speak.

This whole thing about her name. Now that is really unusual, isn't it? We have often laughed about the fact that she never seemed content to have the name, Lori Lynn. It's almost like it didn't really fit her somehow. She was always busy changing her name. I didn't even include the story about her in about third or fourth grade where she came home and decided that she didn't like "Lynn" as her middle name and changed it to "Jane". Again, where she got that, I have no idea. She wanted to be called L J... and that seemed to stick with her. She even had that put on a sweatshirt as her name. The first name we gave her was Christy....you see the word "Christ" in that... but that name didn't stick... interesting!

The first name she called herself was Jello Jones. I was thinking about Jello yesterday... it tends to conform to the mold in which it is placed... so has she... she has conformed to the mold that others around her have placed her in....not good people, mind you... but troubled people have easily influenced her...and she has become what they suggested to her.

Charla Hella... what a name she gave herself... Of course, I see the word Hell in that name... and yes, she has so caused hell in so many lives by her addictive behavior. Isn't it interesting that she chose to hide pills? Pills...under a dresser... out of the view of her parents... especially her Dad... who wanted her healthy and strong by making sure she took vitamins... Perhaps a metaphor for her heavenly Father who she has tried to hide her drug habit from... for so very long... hide those pills... no one will know... no one will see...

Anyway, those are my thoughts right now as I write this. I am amazed at the power of the Holy Spirit as He counsels us... as He teaches us... and I am so blessed by the healing that I am receiving, along with deep spiritual insight... as I write these letters to Lori.

May you be blessed this day also.

CHAPTER SIX
Pain Can Really Hurt!

My dear daughter,

This is all so hard, isn't it? You are finally confined for an extended period of time... your life totally changing and you're not able to escape from this prison sentence. I keep hearing the word "ESCAPE" down in my heart for you. Now, I don't think for a minute that you are trying to literally escape from your jail cell or run, in that way. No, this type of escape is much different. It's actually much more serious that escaping from prison.

Actually, you have been trying to escape for most of your life, haven't you? I remember the first time I saw you in handcuffs. I'm seeing that picture very clearly now as I write this. It was April of 2005 and you had been binging for quite some time on drugs. You had actually run out on your good job as a trainer at a fitness center one Thursday afternoon and decided to escape from the pressures of work and trying to stay clean. When I went to pick you up at work, they said that you had gone for a break that afternoon and never came back. Of course trying to call you on your cell phone brought only a line that sent me directly to voice mail. You must have turned your phone off.

I started calling those that I thought might know where you were. Of course, no one did! I went into the restaurant beside where you worked and asked questions. Actually yes, they knew you and they had seen you get into a taxi that afternoon and drive away. What taxi... what color... what company, I asked. Even with the information that they provided, we were not able to find you. I began to really worry about you... as probably any mother would have done. Where were you? What was going on?   Yes, I did assume that you were probably somewhere doing drugs... but where? Were you safe... were you in danger? All of those questions and more ran through my mind. Family members were called and prayer began to go up for you.   Prayer chains were contacted... friends were asked to pray... all of it. Where was Lori?

Several hours went by. Where do we go to begin to look for you? Since you were now here in Florida with us... trying to start a new life... again... your friends and acquaintances seemed to be few. However, no one knew where you were. Many hours later my phone rang.   It was your best friend,

Marcy... from Indiana. She had talked to you... and yes, you were somewhere doing drugs... and you were telling her that you were going to kill yourself this time. It really was not worth living anymore! She was so convinced that you were serious about suicide that she was screaming and crying into my ear. Something had to be done to find you... she was desperate... and so were we!

I called your brother, Ryan... and he immediately decided to cancel his plans that he had for the weekend and fly down here to help find you. We were all so devastated that we couldn't find you. How could we sleep... or even eat? Where were you? Were you alive... were you laying somewhere dead in some awful alley? Why didn't you care that we would all be searching and praying until you were found? Why didn't that even seem to matter to you, Lori? Yes, your brother dropped everything and came to Florida to help find you. He actually had a friend that was a private investigator... and so the search became more intense. Hours passed by... where were you? Why hadn't you called? We had filled up your voice mail with our pleadings. Why didn't you care enough about all of us to even let us know that you were ok?

As you know, you were found a day or two later... holed up in a drug infested condo... with people laying passed out all over the place. This condo was actually in a decent part of town and the taxi driver had taken you there. This was supposed to be a great party... lots of fun... lots of drugs. You willingly walked into this den of drugs and sin. You didn't seem to care at all that your family and friends would be looking for you and be so concerned about finding you. No, none of that seemed to matter at all, did it? You were going to hang out with these dirty, drugged up people... people you didn't even know... people who didn't care about you... people who were wanting the high... just like you... people who didn't care at all whether you lived or died... people who were also running from their own accountability and responsibility.

Yes, you were found drugged up... not caring about your filthy environment or the people laying around you in their own vomit and filth. Yes, you were found and you had no desire to go with your brother and uncle. But, your uncle... being a big guy... just picked you up and put you over his shoulder... and you, kicking and screaming, were taken out of that hell hole... taken out and given another chance to live... to change... to become all that God wanted you to be. Yes, given yet another chance to live. Yes, you were escaping again...trying to escape into the "nothingness" of your habit...trying to escape from responsibility...a good job...and your family who loved you so much and was trying so hard to help you. Yes, escape is what you did... again!

Ryan and I sat with you at your aunt and uncle's kitchen table. Your situation, your decisions were all discussed. What were YOU going to do about all of this, Lori?

It seemed time to try another rehab program... something more intense... for a longer period of time. Yes, that was the answer. You, however, boldly declared that you were getting on a bus and going back to Indiana... no treatment for you... you were just fine. This was your life and you would decide what to do and where you wanted to live. Of course, this discussion was very intense and you were going to do it "your way" once again. Never mind the danger you had been in... or any of the problems you had caused by your actions... this was your life and you would live it the way you wanted.

And yes, your aunt and uncle, Ryan and I decided to call the sheriff's department and "baker act"you since you were a danger to yourself and others by your threats. As the officers got out of the patrol car, they saw you running up the driveway to the house. You were quickly followed by one of them who saw you stash your drugs in the kitchen garbage can... and the rest of that story unfolded with you being handcuffed after you had kicked my knee in your anger. To see you led away to jail... in handcuffs... was overwhelming and devastating. You could not defend yourself... your hands were behind your back in handcuffs. You were rendered powerless against the strength of the arresting officers. You were bound up... not able to go where you wanted to go... do what you wanted to do. What transpired a few hours later... was even worse. The next morning at your arraignment, in your anger...you stabbed a guard with a ball point pen... in the neck... and found yourself spending the next ten days in the maximum security unit. Had not the officer you stabbed had mercy on you... you would have served a sentence of about a year in Florida for that assault. But again, God had mercy... through that woman... and you were not made to serve that year. To many people that whole experience would have been enough to change the course of their lives forever... for the good, but not you, Lori... no, not you.

And so, you have always been trying to escape. I propose to you, daughter, that you have been trying for so long to escape the pain... the hurt... the disappointments that you have suffered. Many, many people do the same thing. Life deals us some very serious hurts along the way. Many do learn to cope with those hurts... they learn to forgive and go on and receive healing for the pain. You haven't done that... but, now is the time to receive that healing that you so need.

The handcuffs and leg chains certainly bind you up, don't they? You are not free to run and play with your son at the beach... or even come and go as you please. You are bound. You are being held as a prisoner... a prisoner by your own choices, your own decisions.

II Peter 3:9 says "THE LORD IS NOT SLOW ABOUT HIS PROMISE, AS SOME COUNT SLOWNESS, BUT IS PATIENT TOWARD YOU,

NOT WISHING FOR ANY TO PERISH, BUT FOR ALL TO COME TO REPENTANCE."

In the Message Bible that verse says "HE IS RESTRAINING HIMSELF ON ACCOUNT OF YOU, HOLDING BACK THE END BECAUSE HE DOESN'T WANT ANYONE LOST. HE'S GIVING EVERYONE SPACE AND TIME TO CHANGE."

Isn't that wonderful... you have been given the space and time to change. You can shake off the handcuffs and leg irons that have bound you by your choices. In Acts 11:18... Peter talks about the repentance that leads to life. Repentance is simply turning around and going the opposite way... changing your life...renouncing the old way of thinking and living... and starting a new life in God... being totally sorry for the sin and the way you have treated yourself, God and all those around you... it's really making a 180 degree change... turning and going in the opposite direction... from death to life....from drugs to totally living the rest of your life... drug free... !!!!

So often we are not even able to list all the hurts that have contributed to our intense pain. We know we have suffered a lot... but we simply can't remember details or aren't willing to face the situations that hurt us so much. We all have emotional pain... it's what we choose to do with it... that really matters. We can keep it... stuff it down deep within us... and try to ignore it. That's been your choice, hasn't it? The other option is to do it God's way... allowing His blessed Holy Spirit to bring about the healing you so need. He really wants to soothe the pain... bring the understanding... teach you how to forgive all the injustices... He really does want to do all of that for you. However, you must allow that healing to take place within you. You must make the quality decisions necessary to really change this time... change that comes from deep within... change that comes from truly forgiving and healing! That's the kind of change you need. This change is lasting... it can be forever... not temporary. It really can!

I'm reminded of the words of the apostle Paul in I Corinthians 10:13-14:

"NO TEMPTATION HAS OVERTAKEN YOU BUT SUCH AS IS COMMON TO MAN; AND GOD IS FAITHFUL, WHO WILL NOT ALLOW YOU TO BE TEMPTED BEYOND WHAT YOU ARE ABLE, BUT WITH THE TEMPTATION WILL PROVIDE THE WAY OF ESCAPE ALSO, THAT YOU MAY BE ABLE TO ENDURE IT. THEREFORE, MY BELOVED, FLEE FROM IDOLATRY."

Idolatry is anything we put before God... anything that we give the utmost importance in our lives... just as the drugs have been for you... your idol... !

Look at these same words in the Message Bible... very interesting...

"NO TEST OR TEMPTATION THAT COMES OUR WAY IS BEYOND THE COURSE OF WHAT OTHERS HAVE HAD TO FACE. ALL YOU NEED TO REMEMBER IS THAT GOD WILL NEVER LET YOU DOWN; HE'LL NEVER LET YOU BE PUSHED PAST YOUR LIMIT; HE'LL ALWAYS BE THERE TO HELP YOU COME THROUGH IT. SO, MY VERY DEAR FRIENDS, WHEN YOU SEE PEOPLE REDUCING GOD TO SOME-THING THEY AN USE OR CONTROL, GET OUT OT THEIR COMPANY AS FAST AS YOU CAN."

Aren't these interesting words? God will provide the way of escape when the temptation is there. This is good escape... this isn't escaping into the drugs so you won't feel the pain... this is escaping into God who can take away the cravings, changing your desires so that you no longer want to live that same old way. This is escaping into the very presence of God who strengthens you... sustains you... encourages you... gives you new hope and desires. No temptation is too big for God to help you... God will never let you down... He'll always be there to help you... to give you the mental and emotional healing that you need to overcome this awful habit and way of living.

Look at Psalm 18: 20-24 in the Message Bible with me.

"GOD MADE MY LIFE COMPLETE WHEN I PLACED ALL THE PIECES BEFORE HIM. WHEN

I GOT MY ACT TOGETHER, HE GAVE ME A FRESH START. NOW I'M ALERT TO GOD'S WAYS; I DON'T TAKE GOD FOR GRANTED. EVERY DAY I REVIEW THE WAYS HE WORKS; I TRY NOT TO MISS A TRICK. I FEEL PUT BACK TOGETHER, AND I'M WATCHING MY STEP. GOD REWROTE THE TEXT OF MY LIFE WHE I OPENED THE BOOK OF MY HEART TO HIS EYES."

That's the answer, Lori… open the book of your heart to God… to His eyes… He will search you… showing you the hurts and pains of the past… and healing you… as only He can do! A little song is on my heart today for you… here are the words… I'll sing it to you someday…

GOD WILL MAKE A WAY… WHERE THERE SEEMS TO BE NO WAY..

HE WORKS IN WAYS… WE CANNOT SEE… HE WILL MAKE A WAY FOR ME.

HE WILL BE MY GUIDE… HOLD ME CLOSELY TO HIS SIDE… WITH LOVE AND STRENGTH FOR EACH NEW DAY… GOD WILL MAKE A WAY… HE WILL MAKE A WAY.

Yes, God will make a way for you to see your past clearly. He will bring the healing you so need… He will teach you how to forgive… to let go of the past… to truly become the woman that He has planned you to be.

God will change you, daughter... from the inside out... Yes, He can... and Yes, He will! Amen and Amen

I love you so much. I look forward to hearing from you about this process. You are in His hands.

YOUR MOM

Marcia McAllister

CHAPTER SEVEN
It's a Shame to Blame!

Dear Lori,

You are on my mind so much. Of course, there is never a day that goes by but that I wonder how you are doing... how are you feeling? Are you getting settled down some in your new surroundings? Are you spending much time thinking and going over the past and all that was involved with your life as a drug addict? All these things, I wonder.

I wonder if you are really getting the concepts I am writing to you. Are you processing your feelings? Are you looking within and doing the hard work necessary to really change? Are you making the quality decisions to once and for all... change... give up the old lifestyle and all that that would mean for you?

Do you see the need to allow God to really do the work in you that needs to be done? I think about all of this.

It is not easy to talk to you now. We take it all for granted, don't we...the ease with which most of our society can pick up a phone and immediately have the person that they want to talk to on the other line? It's even infinitely easier than it was just 20 years ago...before there were these tiny little cell phones we carry around. It's so easy to just pick one up and dial... but when there is no place to call... no way to reach you... well, that's a completely different story. Of all those cell phones that you have had... and all that I have bought you...you don't have a one now, do you? There is no way for you to reach anyone... without going through the prison phone system... and that's much easier said than done, isn't it?

Last night I got to talk to you for 2 minutes. That seemed so wonderful... just to hear your voice... to hear you say that you were ok... that you were at peace.

I had not heard your voice since the sentencing. Every time we had tried to connect on that system it had booted me out and didn't allow the debit card to work for some reason. We didn't have enough time for me to really talk to you... see how you're coping... what you're thinking. I do appreciate you making the effort to try to make the call... since that must come from your end there in prison.

Actually, daughter... all of this must come from you and from God working in you. It is time for you to make the decision to do what it takes to forever change. I know that I am saying that a lot to you but I feel that you must understand that "the ball is totally in your court." I really think that it always has been. However, as your mama, I couldn't accept that concept... that this lifestyle was your choice and your desire. I have always felt that somehow I was more responsible for all of this than I even knew. I have laid awake countless nights rehearsing events and decisions and wondering what I did to cause you to become a drug addict.

About 8 years ago, after you had run away from my home here in Florida, I decided to face all those feelings of blame. I was blaming myself. I was blaming the divorce that your Dad and I went through back when you were eight years old. I was blaming myself for so many things that I felt that I had done wrong where you were concerned. Now, I can easily get right back into all that self defeating thinking if I want. However, I have learned a few things since 2002 that have helped me understand and cope with your addiction better.

It was December 2002 and I had traveled up to Indiana to spend Christmas with you, your son Levi and his daddy... along with Ryan and his family and your brother Marc. Even though there were good times... especially with all the grandkids... there was that time on Christmas morning where you kept dozing off... actually falling asleep on your sofa as your little son opened his Christmas presents. You really didn't see much of anything that he opened and you certainly were not capable of playing with any of his new toys with him.

You were not able to open any presents yourself... as you were drugged up. I'm not sure all that you had in your system that day... but suffice it to say... you were very much "out of it". You would wake up half way for a moment or two... and then slump back down into the sofa for hours at a time. Yes, we had Christmas without you. Now that scene has continued to play out again and again through the years. You really seem to get yourself all drugged up for important events and holidays, don't you? Not that you haven't been drugged on a regular basis for almost twenty years now....but I have noticed that you are even worse off when there is a designated time for family holidays and birthdays. Even this past year at Christmas with your Dad's family I was told how you slept on the sofa while Levi and everyone else opened presents, ate and had a good time together. But where was Lori? Asleep...out of it, as usual. Why is that, Lori?

I propose to you that holidays and events like that are somehow painful to you. Perhaps they remind you of times when life wasn't as perfect as we would have liked it to be. We were not the "Beaver Cleaver" family of TV sitcom days. Actually, we were probably more typical of many families that were going through difficult emotional upsets in the home and marriage. Even though others were suffering some of the same scenarios, that knowledge doesn't really help us cope with the pain that we were suffering. I will be the first to admit that my marriage to your Dad did not turn out the way I had intended. When I married him in 1968, I couldn't imagine living a day without him. It was all wonderful... all such happiness... for awhile.

I will not go into detail at all about the fifteen years of our marriage. There were some wonderful times... especially when all three of you were born. You are all the joy of my life. I would do it all again to have you all. I thank God for your Dad and the good times... the joy of establishing a home and a family... all of it. However, our time together was also filled with much pain.

Unfortunately you all heard arguments, saw fights and misunderstandings that I wished then... and now... I could have kept from you. However, that is life. Life can be very painful and at times, ugly and mean. Through it all, neither your Dad or I have ever stopped loving all of you. We are grateful for you and both of us so wish you had not gone through all your drug abuse and suffering, Lori.

I'm now seeing a scene that happened to you when you were nine years old. It was summer and your Dad was getting ready to remarry. You decided to get all dressed up and be a part of the wedding to his young bride. Your brothers refused to even go to the wedding... let alone be in it and a part of the bridal party. Not you... you wanted to please your Dad... and you also enjoyed getting all dressed up for special occasions. But this was quite a different occasion, wasn't it? You talked later about how strange it was to be standing up there in front of that church with your Dad and the woman that was about to become his new wife and a step-mother to you. However you wanted to make your Dad happy and so you not only went to the wedding but you were a part of it. Later that evening your grandparents brought you home and we all sat around and talked and ate popcorn together. Even that was almost surreal... your Dad had just married someone else and we all sat around and talked and ate popcorn!

It was very difficult for all of us, including your grandparents to really deal with all that had happened. We just went on... we just moved on with our lives... or did we? Did you? In all likelihood, all the pain of the divorce and life after that event began to catch up with you... along with much more. I can't even begin to speculate about all the events that came together to contribute to your addiction... but I do know that all of this was a factor somehow. Pray about all of this... God will minister to you and bring the forgiveness and soothe the pain of your past, daughter. Yes, He will do that for you!

So who is to blame for all your pain? For years I seemed to take the blame of it all on myself. I could go into great detail describing to you why I thought it was all my fault. Yes, I could blame your Dad some, too. To describe any of that would serve no point. My point here is that to play the blame game only ends up in more pain and suffering. It never makes you feel better to point the finger of blame at anyone... including and especially ... yourself.

After your obviously drugged up Christmas vacation in 2002, I decided to bring you back to Florida with me and put you into a Christian drug rehabilitation center. I know you remember those events. However, you didn't remember much of our drive back to Florida. As we pulled through a drive through a few blocks from your home in Indiana as we were getting ready to hit the road, you ordered your meal and as you opened your sandwich in your lap, you fell sound asleep with your face in your food... without eating a bite. You had obviously taken something again... something to make you feel better, I presumed. And so you traveled much of the way back to Florida with me... asleep.

A couple of days later you were admitted to the Christian rehab only to have you cross their boundary lines and walk away from the help that they would have provided. Yes, you called me from a pay phone that you had walked to... on that warm Florida January day... and then we were back to square one again... as we had been so many times through the years. We could talk about many, many similar scenarios like this, couldn't we? But then, what good would it really do to rehash all the disappointments of failed treatment for you? It would only serve to point out how very much we wanted you to be helped and how much you had defied us and any other authority and again and refused the treatment that was offered to you.

Through the years there has been a resounding theme from you about your addiction. I have heard it many times directed at me. I'm sure you have also felt many feelings toward others in the family... and even yourself. That central theme is "the blame game". When attempts have been made at counseling and treatment, many times issues have come up and opportunities for blame have presented themselves. It seems to be a human condition to try to place blame on others... more than ourselves... when forced to look at the pain of our actions. The lifestyle that you have led all these years has caused tremendous problems and pain in your family... but especially with your young son... and for you!

One of the major themes that I keep saying to you in my letters is that of forgiveness. Again, you can't go back and change what has happened. You can't second guess the self-destructive actions you have taken so many times. You can't take away the pain that you have caused all those who love you so much. All that has happened... those are facts. However, you can change the outcome of those actions by changing yourself... actually allowing God to change you... once and for all. I believe that God has given you this time... these years in prison now... to really allow you the opportunity for total change. That total change starts with forgiveness and dealing with the shame of your past.

Again, forgiveness does not mean we agree with what was done....whether by us or someone doing something that hurt us. Forgiveness is an act of your will... not your feelings... forgiveness says..."you don't owe me anymore... I cancel the debt that you have with me... I let it go... I allow God to change my feelings as I make the decision to forgive for the action that hurt me."

These can be things that you have done that have settled within you as remorse, guilt and shame. Many of the things that you need to forgive are probably things you have done to hurt others. Now is the time to let it all go... give up the shame and stop blaming yourself and even others for the wrong decisions you have made.

When you have been in the center of your addiction... actively using and not even trying to get help or curb the problem, it has seemed to me that you don't even care about the feelings of others around you... especially your son. You are "hell bent" on doing the drugs... on finding them... on doing what you want to do...when you want to do it. Never mind that you have had jobs, responsibilities of a young child, and countless other things that you should have been doing instead of feeding your habit. All of this has been self centeredness... with capital letters! It has been ALL ABOUT YOU... all about YOUR next high... all about escaping into YOUR addiction... all about forgetting for a time that YOU do have responsibilities. This has been your life for so much of the past twenty years. What will your life look like for the next twenty... or fifty years?

Yes, God, in His amazing mercy, is giving you another opportunity to give up that old lifestyle of running... running from your pain... running from your responsibilities... running from the shame... running from all the resentment and anger... all of it. He is giving you quiet time... away from the many voices that have influenced you so much through the years. Those voices were wanting you to join in the "high"... forget your daily commitments... just get away and escape once again. Those voices did not and still don't... by the way... have your best interests at stake... oh, no... THOSE VOICES ARE OUT TO TAKE YOU OVER... USE YOU... CONTROL YOU AND NOT ALLOW YOU TO BECOME ALL THAT GOD HAS PLANNED FOR YOU. Those voices have been boyfriends... countless boyfriends... that said they loved you... wanted to make a home with you... and all the other lies they told you. Those voices have been friends that said that you are so much fun to party with... so let's go... let's leave work... let's just disappear for a few hours... all of it. Those voices are the voices of DEATH... not life. Those voices have come disguised as friends, lovers and buddies. Those voices have been put in your path to bring you totally down... actually to kill you!

HERE is the most important voice in all of time and place ...the voice of God... God Almighty... and He is using His Word to say this to you.

ISAIAH 41:10: "DO NOT FEAR, FOR I AM WITH YOU; DO NOT ANXIOUSLY LOOK ABOUT YOU, SURELY I WILL HELP YOU. SURELY I WILL UPHOLD YOU WITH MY RIGHTEOUS RIGHT HAND"...

ISAIAH 54:4: "FEAR NOT, FOR YOU WILL NOT BE PUT TO SHAME; NEITHER FEEL HUMILIATED, FOR YOU WILL NOT BE DISGRACED; BUT YOU WILL FORGET THE SHAME OF YOUR YOUTH"...

ISAIAH 53:4-6... Message Bible... "BUT THE FACT IS, IT WAS OUR PAINS HE CARRIED—OUR DISFIGUREMENTS, ALL THE THINGS WRONG WITH US. WE THOUGHT HE BROUGHT IT ON HIMSELF, THAT GOD WAS PUNISHING HIM FOR HIS OWN FAILURES. BUT IT WAS OUR SINS THAT DID THAT TO HIM, THAT RIPPED AND TORE AND CRUSHED HIM---OUR SINS! HE TOOK THE PUNISHMENT, AND THAT MADE US

WHOLE. THROUGH HIS BRUISES WE GET HEALED. WE'RE ALL LIKE SHEEP WHO'VE WANDERED OFF AND GOTTEN LOST. WE'VE ALL DONE OUR OWN THING...GONE OUR OWN WAY. AND GOD HAS PILED ALL OUR SINS, EVERYTHING WE'VE DONE WRONG, ON HIM, ON HIM."

Aren't those powerful words? We're like sheep who've wandered off and gotten lost... "LITTLE GIRL LOST"... that's been you, daughter. That's in the title of this book... "Little Girl Lost"... but you don't have to stay LOST... that's the good news! You are found... if you really choose to be found... You are saved from all that would have had you... that would have killed you... if you really choose to be saved from it all. You've done your own thing... gone your own way... and God has taken all your sin... all your sin... all of it... and piled it on Jesus on the cross. You no longer have to carry it... be ashamed of it... or try to blame others for it. It has been dealt with on the cross... all the shame... all the guilt... all the sin. It can be forever gone... forever on Him... no longer on you... no longer on you to carry around... it can be forever on Him...

IF YOU ALLOW HIM TO HAVE IT ALL... IF YOU MAKE THE QUALITY DECISIONS TO REPENT OF IT ALL... GIVE IT ALL TO JESUS... YOUR DRUG HABIT... AND YOUR CRAZY THINKING... YOUR MANY HURTFUL ACTIONS... ALL OF IT...

JUST GIVE IT TO HIM TODAY AS YOU READ THESE WORDS.

Make the decision to no longer carry all that sin… all those wrong decisions. Give it all to Jesus… and He will turn your sorrow into joy!

Psalm 30:5…..

"HIS FAVOR IS FOR A LIFE-TIME; WEEPING MAY LAST FOR THE NIGHT, BUT A SHOUT OF JOY COMES IN THE MORNING."

Psalm 30: 10-12:

"HEAR, O LORD, AND BE GRACIOUS TO ME; O LORD, BE THOU MY HELPER." THOU HAST TURNED FOR ME MY MOURNING INTO DANCING; THOU HAS LOOSED MY SACKCLOTH AND GIRDED ME WITH GLADNESS; THAT MY SOUL MAY SING PRAISE TO THEE, AND NOT BE SILENT. O LORD MY GOD, I WILL GIVE THANKS TO THEE FOREVER.

It's really an amazing, totally miraculous thing that God does for us… when we are really sincere about changing. You sent some letters to me in an envelope recently for me to hold for you… and then return to you someday. One of those letters was from an old boyfriend who contributed to all the problems you found yourself in… here in Florida. As I read his words to you, I realized that his supposed change…

his repentance... his turning his life around... has not happened. He had written me a letter a few weeks ago... all about his changes... all about what God has done in him. As I read the words he sent me, I found myself thinking..."this is not true... this is all a lie... something is not right here." And now, reading his words to you, Lori... I have seen again this man's lies... his real heart attitudes and desires. He does not have your best interest at heart... He is still using... and still in agreement with the drug addicted lifestyle. You will have many voices like this, daughter... voices that try so hard to influence you. The choice is yours.   God can... and He so wants to... do a miracle in your life NOW... will you let Him... or will you continue to buy all the lies?

This choice is before you... life or death... choose life!

DEUTERONOMY 30:19-20   "I CALL HEAVEN AND EARTH TO WITNESS AGAINST YOU TODAY, THAT I HAVE SET BEFORE YOU LIFE AND DEATH, THE BLESSING AND THE CURSE. SO CHOOSE LIFE IN ORDER THAT YOU MAY LIVE, YOU AND YOUR DESCENDANTS, BY LOVING THE LORD YOUR GOD, BY OBEYING HIS VOICE, AND BY HOLDING FAST TO HIM; FOR THIS IS YOUR LIFE AND THE LENGTH OF YOUR DAYS, THAT YOU MAY LIVE IN THE LAND WHICH THE LORD SWORE TO YOUR FATHERS..."

I love you so much, daughter... and I pray for you even now as I write these words that your CHOICE IS LIFE... no longer to go back to those old ways of living... this is your new day... grab it... take it... make the right decisions... today!

YOUR MOM...
who loves you so very much.

CHAPTER EIGHT
From Mad to Glad!

Dear daughter,

Today I am thinking about you and praying that all is going well... as well as can be expected in your situation.   I hope to hear from you soon and I check my mailbox everyday wondering if there will be a letter from you. Your recent comment to me in one of your letters about "me not being 30 anymore and I should not work so many long hours..."   I understand... and appreciate. However, there is so much to get done... not just with my daily real estate job... but especially in the ministry.   There are so many people that are hurting... many that are even going through similar situations that we are all going through, with you.   There are so many out there that need hope... need God's guidance and wisdom... and especially need to know that addicts can, indeed, change and turn their lives around.

Are you one of those addicts, Lori... who can really change and put the old life behind you? I know that you can... but are you willing to do the hard work necessary to make the changes deep within yourself? For twenty years you have managed to "play the game"..."play the system"...and "play all those around you". Actually, you are quite good at all of that... of manipulating people and situations to get what you want. Even though this all may be hard for you to hear, you do need to hear it, so please take all this very seriously.

Through all these many years with you, I have grown accustomed to many patterns of behavior that you have exhibited. Those of us in your family that have dealt with all of this have gotten very well acquainted with your lying. Now, I mean to call it... LYING... because it is. It's not just telling part of the truth or changing parts of an event or situation to meet your needs. It is actually downright LYING, isn't it? It has become such a way of life for you that I propose to you that even you sometimes aren't sure what is the truth and what is a lie. Would you agree with that?

Just a few months back... December and January... you were telling me on the phone that you were going to outpatient therapy, getting your drug tests, trying to find a job again and much more. Actually, I later found out when you were arrested again at the end of January, that you had not been going to your probation   meetings...   you   were   not   going   to outpatient therapy... you were not getting the regular mandatory drug screening... on and on... and on. All that you said you were doing... you were not actually doing at all! Yes, this habit of lying... trying to cover up the real truth... has been a HUGE problem for you for so many years now that it appears this has become a big part of who you are.

You have had more jobs that I can even begin to list. I'm sure you can't list them either. I told you recently in a letter that I'm sure you could not begin to put down on paper all the places you have ever lived and the people who have lived there with you. In so many of those situations... when your life suddenly changed again... you had a story about the events leading up to the change. In many of those instances, I was later able to learn that you had been lying, yet again, about the real reasons for the changes you had made.

Without belaboring this point, I want to talk to you today about the real Lori... the inside of you... your character... what makes you ... YOU. How have you reacted so consistently in your lifetime when you don't get your way... when the events don't go the way you want them to go? Do you just try to understand a situation, a person's decisions you don't like... can you "roll with the punches"... accept that life doesn't always give the results we want? If you're totally honest with yourself, you must admit that you are so very often filled with deep anger and resentment when you don't get your way. Now, you may be thinking, as you read this... that I am really coming down hard on you... and yes, I am. It is very hard for a parent to sit by and watch a child... no matter how old or how young... self destruct. It is not usually in the heart of a parent to want harm or danger to come to that child, is it?

All of that has brought me to this point in my life where I find you locked up in prison for an extended period of time... and me here wondering what I can do to genuinely help you. Here it is... I must, as your mother... tell it like it is, Lori. I must try my best to help you... and allow God's Holy Spirit to minister truth to you as you read... and re-read... all these words that I am consistently sending to you. I must trust that God, who loves you so very much, and I are a team in this with you. God's heart, like mine, is to help you... to have compassion on you and point you in the right direction, giving you wisdom to make the right choices from now on in your life.

Yes, you are at THE BIG CROSSROADS in your life! As I was reading your ex-boyfriend's words to you in a letter you sent me, I saw the pattern of behavior that so many addicts have. It is... do the time... stay out of trouble in prison... then get out and do "drugs in moderation", "fly under the radar"... so as not to get caught. That is exactly what he said to you. That's what he is doing... and that is the way he expects you to live when you get out of prison. Really?... Really, Lori? This man cannot be allowed to influence you. This married man with a young son is promising you a life when you get out... that's ridiculous. He is still using and will drag you down even further than you have ever been if you go back to all of that with him. This is the man who had you stealing from stores here with him and contributed greatly to you doing crack, cocaine and so much more. This is that man, Lori. You must take your stand against his influence and his evil suggestions to you. He brings with him danger, deceit and drugs... and quite possibly death.

Daughter, You have so much more going for you... than all of that. You really are gifted, sweet, intelligent, compassionate and have a heart after God. You are not destined to just "maintain your drug habit... under the radar". God has so much more for you than a life of drugs, deceit and chaos.

I believe that it is time to expose all the underlying anger and lying. I believe it's time to call it all for what it is... a deadly way to live. Your best friend Marcy is no longer on this earth, is she, Lori? She was killed a couple years back in a terrible truck accident with her drug addicted husband driving. Fortunately her baby was saved... remained barely scratched... but now lives WITHOUT her mother... forever. Marcy would have preferred to live and raise her beautiful little girl... but she was not allowed to do so. Her husband took her life. This is the man that supposedly loved her. Please look at this and ask yourself is this truly what you want for your life and Levi?

Lori, I really think that if Marcy had lived through that terrible wreck, she would have been very outspoken about the wreck and how dangerous it was for her husband to be using drugs and driving. I don't think Marcy would have taken any of that lightly. Her little daughter could have been killed… and she WAS killed. She would have continued to warn you about the drug use and the men you were spending time with. These types of men are out to completely control their girlfriends or wives. The goal is to isolate you from your family that loves you. I have seen this for years with you and the men with whom you have been involved. There seems to be no respect for your family and those trying to help you. These men are out to control you… use you… and ruin your life. Even this letter from this ex-boyfriend shows all of this. His utter disrespect for me as your mother… his attitude about what life will be like when you are out of prison… all of it… is alarming and very sad.

Look at the words in I Corinthians chapter 13 in the Message Bible about the true meaning of love… what it is…and what it should look like in our lives.

 I Corinthians 13: 4-7:

"SO, NO MATTER WHAT I SAY, WHAT I BELIEVE, AND WHAT I DO, I'M BANKRUPT WITHOUT LOVE.

LOVE NEVER GIVES UP.

LOVE CARES MORE FOR OTHERS THAN FOR SELF.

LOVE DOESN'T WANT WHAT IT DOESN'T HAVE.

LOVE DOESN'T STRUT, DOESN'T HAVE A SWELLED HEAD.

DOESN'T FORCE ITSELF ON OTHERS,

ISN'T ALWAYS "ME FIRST"

DOESN'T FLY OFF THE HANDLE,

DOESN'T KEEP SCORE OF THE SINS OF OTHERS.

DOESN'T REVEL WHEN OTHERS GROVEL,

TAKES PLEASURE IN THE FLOWERING OF TRUTH,

PUTS UP WITH ANYTHING.

TRUSTS GOD ALWAYS.

ALWAYS LOOKS FOR THE BEST,

NEVER LOOKS BACK,

BUT KEEPS GOING TO THE END.

LOVE NEVER DIES."

That, my daughter, is LOVE. Love is not what you have been living with so many people for so many years. It is time to really look at your past relationships and set some standards for yourself and future relationships. What do you want to see in the one who professes to really love you? Never settle for a fake... or a liar! This is too serious for you from now on. It's time to make quality decisions about the ones that you are the closest to in the future.

I heard a psychologist talking yesterday on the "Today Show". She said that abusive boyfriends and husbands don't respect women at all. They are out to destroy the relationship and the person that they are with. Look at this statement that she made. I think it is very profound... "LOVE IS A BEHAVIOR... NOT A FEELING!" It's how a person treats you... not what words they say... that proves their love for you. You have been addicted to abusive men all your life. You seem to always find the worst "scumbags"... and yes, I said that word... scumbags... to be with. I remember so many of the men that you have been with, Lori. Most of them had the trait of being a "user and abuser." I could write a whole chapter or more on all of that. Suffice it to say, you deserve more than that. You deserve someone who will treat you with love... not just say the words... "I love you"... but someone who will indeed live that love on a daily basis. Offering you a life of drugs... under the radar... is not love at all. It is living a lie... living a life of destruction and death. It is a total control issue, not love, nor respect. All of that is offering you a life that will eventually... sooner or later... kill you. Do you want that... not only for yourself... but for your precious little Levi? Do you?

Actually, Lori I think it is time to completely get people, like this man we're talking about here, out of your life once and for all.   There must be NO more communication with those that would drag you back into that drugging, drinking and partying lifestyle. You and I have discussed this concept for years now. It is those around you... those strong voices in your life... that have contributed so profoundly to your habitual and destructive behavior.

Take a look at these words about love found in I John 4:7-8

"MY BELOVED FRIENDS, LET US CON-TINUE TO LOVE EACH OTHER SINCE LOVE COMES FROM GOD. EVERYONE WHO LOVES IS BORN OF GOD AND EXPERIENCES A RELATIONSHIP WITH GOD. THE PERSON WHO REFUSES TO LOVE DOESN'T KNOW THE FIRST THING ABOUT GOD, BECAUSE GOD IS LOVE--SO YOU CAN'T KNOW HIM IF YOU DON'T LOVE."

Haven't treatment centers all told you that you must change the people you associate with if you are going to stay clean? The answer is YES... you must realize the danger and death that people like this bring to you.   You cannot walk around in a daze... just having your own way... living this lifestyle and not really seeing what these people who have used you and abused you... are all about. I know you see it... we have discussed it for years.

Not only do these people bring you more opportunities to get the drugs you have wanted... but also, I believe they contribute tremendously to your anger and lying. They promote hatred for those who truly love you. They have burned bridges in their lives with family and friends and all of that has so often resulted in deep seated anger, resentment and yes, hatred. They have influenced you... they have added to your anger and helped to strengthen all the negative behaviors, haven't they?

Look at these words found in the book of Proverbs... words of wisdom for you to really study and memorize. These verses will help you see clearly when people like this are trying to influence you.

Proverbs 22:24-25: Message Bible...
"DON'T HANG OUT WITH ANGRY PEOPLE; DON'T KEEP COMPANY WITH HOT-HEADS. BAD TEMPER IS CONTAGIOUS—DON'T GET INFECTED."

These same words in the New American Standard Bible say this:

"DO NOT ASSOCIATE WITH A MAN GIVEN TO ANGER; OR GO WITH A HOT-TEMPERED MAN,

LEST YOU LEARN HIS WAYS AND FIND A SNARE FOR YOURSELF."

Also, look at these wise words from the book of Proverbs... which, by the way, you need to be reading and reading... and studying and memorizing, in order to help you stay out of trouble there in prison and also when you are released.

Proverbs 10:6: "BLESSINGS ACCRUE ON A GOOD AND HONEST LIFE, BUT THE MOUTH OF THE WICKED IS A DARK CAVE OF ABUSE."
The Message Bible

Proverbs 10: 9-12: "HONESTY LIVES CONFIDENT AND CAREFREE, BUT SHIFTY IS SURE TO BE EXPOSED. AN EVASIVE EYE IS A SIGN OF TROUBLE AHEAD, BUT AN OPEN, FACE-TO-FACE MEETING RESULTS IN PEACE. THE MOUTH OF A GOOD PERSON IS A DEEP, LIFE-GIVING WELL, BUT THE MOUTH OF THE WICKED IS A DARK CAVE OF ABUSE. HATRED STARTS FIGHTS, BUT LOVE PULLS A QUILT OVER THE BICKERING." Message Bible

Proverbs 12: 14-22: "WELL-SPOKEN WORDS BRING SATISFACTION; WELL-DONE WORK HAS ITS OWN REWARD. FOOLS ARE HEADSTRONG AND DO WHAT THEY LIKE; WISE PEOPLE TAKE ADVICE. FOOLS HAVE SHORT FUSES AND EXPLODE ALL TOO QUICKLY; THE PRUDENT QUIETLY SHRUG OFF IN-SULTS. TRUTHFUL

WITNESS BY A GOOD PERSON CLEARS THE AIR, BUT LIARS LAY DOWN A SMOKE SCREEN OF DECEIT. RASH LANGUAGE CUTS AND MAIMS, BUT THERE IS HEALING IN THE WORDS OF THE WISE. TRUTH LASTS; LIES ARE HERE TODAY, GONE TO-MORROW. EVIL SCHEMING DISTORTS THE SCHEMER; PEACE-PLANNING BRINGS JOY TO THE PLANNER. NO EVIL CAN OVERWHELM A GOOD PERSON, BUT THE WICKED HAVE THEIR HANDS FULL OF IT. GOD CAN'T STOMACH LIARS; HE LOVES THE COMPANY OF THOSE WHO KEEP THEIR WORD."
The Message Bible

Well, I couldn't begin to say all that... that eloquently. There it is in black and white for you to read and digest. Lori, this is all so serious. This aspect of your past life... all the anger, hatred, lying, deceit... all of it must be gone from you... for good. This is no casual conversation about learning not to lie. This is again... LIFE OR DEATH TO YOU. This is so serious. You must look at all of this and repent... turn away from all these deadly attitudes and actions and turn to God to help you no longer desire all the lying, stealing, anger, resentment, hatred... all of that package. God can deliver you from all of it... HE CAN TAKE AWAY THE DESIRE TO BE AROUND PEOPLE LIKE THIS! He can show you a better way to live. He can do it! Will you work with Him to really recognize all of this in yourself and others? When you see it... really see it... you will also be able to finally understand how very destructive for you and your son... all of this truly is.

My prayer for you today is that you will take all that I have said to you very seriously. I pray that you will see and hear God's voice in these words and realize that you have been given another opportunity to really change... to really allow God to take away all the anger, resentment, hatred... lying... all of it! These attitudes cannot be hidden. They are exposed for what they really are... all death to you. May God be very close to you today... helping you hear His voice... teaching you how to give all of this up... once and for all... and then training you to become so filled up with Him that you are indeed a new person... a child of His... and of mine... that really and sincerely desires to be all that God wants you to be. It is then, Lori... that you will truly be able to turn all the MAD... all the anger and hatred package... into GLAD... from sorrow to joy... there it is again...

Psalm 30: 11-12: "HEAR, O LORD, AND BE GRACIOUS TO ME; O LORD, BE THOU MY HELPER," THOU HAST TURNED FOR ME MY MOURNING INTO DANCING; THOU HAST LOOSED MY SACKCLOTH AND GIRDED ME WITH GLADNESS; THAT MY SOUL MAY SING PRAISE TO THEE, AND NOT BE SILENT, O LORD MY GOD, I WILL GIVE THANKS TO THEE FOREVER." NASB translation

I know you can do this, daughter. I love you so much and I am here for you.   I hope to hear from you soon.

YOUR MOM

CHAPTER NINE
False Evidence Appearing Real

Dear Lori,

How are you today?   Are you beginning to work on the serious subjects we are discussing in these letters? Are you finding yourself desiring a better life than you had in the past, when you are finally released from prison?   I hope you are taking the time to read all of these letters over and over again.   I want these talks... via letter... to help you make the changes you so need to make in your life.

You have asked about my little doggies, Bailey Boy and Zoe Grace.   Yes, they miss you and I tell them that you love and miss them, too.   Last night when I was taking them out before bedtime, I was thinking about you... wondering how you are really coping with your environment there.   I began to wonder if you ever get really afraid. That thought came to me as, once again, Bailey and Zoe began to bark at nothing... just the night sounds of the wind in the palm trees. There were no cars going by... there really was no one talking in their driveway... or any other dogs barking. It was very quiet and peaceful... until... until they thought they heard something. You could see both of them become instantly frightened. They were barking that "fearful bark" that they sometimes do. Actually, Zoe started it...as she often does, and then Bailey hearing her bark, immediately began to panic and barked very loudly. How difficult it is to get them to calm down when they perceive a sudden scary sound or anticipate someone coming toward them in the dark!

Fear of the unknown... fear of something or someone coming to hurt us... fear of something we cannot even see... all of this... this huge mountain of fear has been your life for so long, hasn't it? Perhaps fear of not being able to get the next fix... quick enough... fear of getting "bad drugs" that could kill you... fear of the police catching up with you and arresting you for all that you were doing... all the constant living in fear... and for what? You have suffered so needlessly, Lori. Fear is crippling... fear is not your friend. Fear is debilitating. Fear can be paralyzing.

All of this reminds me of your way of life for so many years. I can't imagine how scary it must have been to know that you needed the drugs... needed to find some quickly... and then put yourself in very scary situations with mean and dangerous people... just to get your fix. All of that is a very horrendous and fearful way to live... not at all a life of peace and security... but instead, a life on the run. That life is behind you now... and must continue to be behind you forever. That life will   KILL YOU if you return to it.

This is not original with me... but I love this description of F.E.A.R... FALSE EVIDENCE APPEARING REAL! Isn't that true? So often what seems to be true... what seems to be reality... is not reality at all. These GIANTS in our lives... those self-concepts... those feelings about ourselves... those ways of thinking that would try to control us and ruin us... are all out there... waiting to scare us... just like the imaginary figures in the dark for Bailey and Zoe.

Actually, they are within you... not just out there waiting to get you, if you will. They are working in your mind and emotions to bring you down... to cripple you and cause you to not fight them... but instead, to give in to them. They are so deceiving... so controlling. They tell you that you are not able to amount to much of anything... so why not just drug yourself up and escape from the reality of life? They tell you that you are not smart enough or "together" enough to get a really good job that will make you truly happy and productive. They tell you that you are not a good mother... never will be a good mother... so why really try, anyway? They even tell you that you cannot stay clean for any length of time at all... that you are simply an addict... a drug addict... that you must have the drugs... you cannot live without them... you cannot face life's situations without all the drugs.   Does any of that sound familiar to you? I know it does.

All of these voices have a strong similarity that seems to hold them all together... the root is FEAR. Again, fear is best described as FALSE EVIDENCE APPEARING REAL... fear is that voice that gives you "FALSE" statements... lies, if you will, that attempt to ruin you... to bring you down... to tell you that you are LESS THAN... less than your brothers, for instance... or your cousins... and countless others in your life. "False evidence"... something presented to you that is not true at all... but appears to be true. Too often we buy the lie... make it our own.

More than likely there are many such fears that are harassing you. Perhaps... fear of failure, fear of trying to live without the drugs, fear of not being able to get a decent job... and keep it, fear of not being able to face the issues you need to face in order to stay clean, fear of the future when you are released from prison, fear, fear, fear...

Now, God says that there is an answer to all this fear. Of course, He talks about it in His Word to us. You know, I often wonder how people, who don't take the Word seriously, actually conquer fear. It seems that they probably try to "talk themselves into courage"... maybe "pump themselves up... that everything will be ok...no need to be afraid of the future..." and then, life happens... as it always does... and then there is new cause to fear... to wonder how they will make it through yet another very stressful or hurtful situation. Without God, I don't know how the average person does make it through all the hassles that life brings.

A few days ago, a very good friend of mine called me with something that I needed to hear. She felt like God was speaking to her to give me a couple of verses to ponder. She knows about your situation and has prayed with me for you on numerous occasions. Those verses are Luke 8:49-50 and they say this, in the New American Standard Bible:

"WHILE HE WAS STILL SPEAKING, SOMEONE CAME FROM THE HOUSE OF THE SYNAGOGUE OFFICIAL SAYING, "YOUR DAUGHTER HAS DIED; DO NOT TROUBLE THE TEACHER ANYMORE." BUT WHEN JESUS HEARD THIS, HE ANSWERED HIM, "DO NOT BE AFRAID ANY LONGER; ONLY BELIEVE, AND SHE SHALL BE MADE WELL."

Lori, those verses can also pertain to you. When my friend read me the verses, my heart was encouraged and uplifted. "DO NOT BE AFRAID ANY LONGER...ONLY BELIEVE... AND SHE SHALL BE MADE WELL." AMEN AND AMEN! I knew she was right. These verses are sent from God for us... for me... to not fear, and instead, let God do the work in you that needs to be done... and for you, to reassure you that He does see your situation and is changing you... making YOU whole!

FEAR IS THE OPPOSITE OF FAITH !!!! Look at that statement over and over again. When we are bogged down in fear... we certainly don't seem to have much faith working in us. Instead, we are thinking about all the "WHAT IFs" that come bombarding us in our minds. What if Lori wants to remain an addict and never decides to change? What if she prefers that awful lifestyle to one of becoming all she can be in God? The "WHAT IFs" in our lives are devastating... they can control us... they can ruin any chance of real change that we have. They can destroy us with their ideas of what MIGHT happen. They can certainly take away any peace of mind that we might be experiencing. The "WHAT Ifs" must be destroyed as soon as they are recognized!

As I write this, I'm remembering a scene that happened in our family when I was about 11 or 12 years old. As you know, your grandparents took my sisters and me to the mission field in Guatemala and we were living there for a few years... in rather primitive conditions, by U.S. standards. Grandpa felt the call of God on his life very strongly back in 1958 and decided that he must fulfill that call, regardless of what his parents or siblings thought about that decision. He was a successful pastor at a growing country church in Indiana when God called him to pick us all up and move us to Central America so that he and your Grandma could fulfill the call that God had given them to become missionaries in that foreign land.

One day, my sisters, Karen and Jan and I were playing on the patio. We were shocked to look up and see this creature crawling toward us. It was a large snake. I don't know what kind it was... but it seemed huge. We started to scream and your Grandpa heard us from his office in the front of the house. He came running. He didn't walk slowly and take his time asking us what the problem was. He immediately heard the panic in our screams and heard the word "snake". He grabbed his MACHETE... the one I still have on my bookcase today. He pulled the long knife out of the holder and ran TOWARD that big old ugly snake. You see, that snake was endangering his family... his three little daughters. He did not stand idly by and talk to the snake and make friends with him.

Your Grandpa had a sudden burst of energy and desire to do something about this huge threat. He ran right TO the snake and began to cut it up into a great number of pieces... he just chopped it up... like you would cut a carrot or a potato. He chopped it up so fast that we were hardly able to take it all in. The threat was immediately over... the snake was very dead... and we were all safe. End of story... He rushed TO the threat... met it head on... did not back off until he had conquered the enemy. I know you loved your Grandpa so much and he prayed for years for you... and would still be doing it if he weren't in heaven now rejoicing around the throne of God. His prayer and desire for you always was that you would overcome this awful disease... that you would fulfill the call on your life that God placed there so many years ago. Grandpa and I had many talks about you and he knew that you were special and that God has big plans for you. He also knew that the devil was fighting you hard... trying to keep you from becoming the ambassador for Jesus that was planned for you.

Daughter, I see you running TO the problems in your life... and overcoming them. I really do. I wouldn't be taking all this time to write so many extensive letters to you if I thought there was no hope for you. You are much like your Grandpa. He was a very compassionate man with a heart after God. He loved people and he had such a way of helping people. When we lived in Chiquimula, Guatemala and I was in the ninth grade taking all my classes through correspondence from the University of Nebraska, I was with him everyday... along with your precious Grandma. I walked with Grandpa in the Bible School... watched him interact with his pastoral students that he taught. I went with him to the villages to preach and watched him lay hands on people for healing. I heard him preach his heart out... all about the mercy and forgiveness of the Lord. I watched him live all that he preached. As you know, he was a man of great love and compassion. He was also a man of laughter and joy... wasn't he? He never met a stranger. He loved people instantly and accepted them for who they were. He was truly a soldier in the Lord's army. This was a true man of God!

Lori, you have inherited so many of Grandpa's traits. I have seen them in you since you were a little girl. You also never meet a stranger. You are instantly able to make conversation and let that person know that you care about them. You do have a heart after God... just like your precious Grandpa. He was never afraid to fulfill the call that God had on his life... regardless of how hard his parents tried to get him to change his mind about taking Grandma and his three little daughters to a foreign land. He was determined to serve God... determined with all his heart!! He always told me that the ministry is the hardest job ... you will ever LOVE. He said if God has called you... you simply must do what He says... or you will be running from him all your life.

You have been running, Lori... You have been running all your life. You have been afraid ... afraid that you were not adequate... afraid that you were not "all that"! You have been afraid to make the commitment to God... to be clean ... to be used of God for wonderful things. Yes, you have been filled with fear. It is now time... during this quiet time in your life... to run toward that fear. Destroy it with the power of your decisions and your speaking and believing what God has said about you. For way too long you have believed the lie... allowed the lie of the devil to control you and stop you from your calling. You have bought the lie, hook... line and sinker, so to speak. You have bought the lie, daughter. That huge garbage bag of lies has tried to destroy you... and tried to take your calling that God has placed within you. That lie must be stopped. Remember, God doesn't call the equipped, but rather equips the called, so you must stop the lie by the confession of your mouth... by learning the Word... by making quality decisions to no longer even entertain for a moment that old lifestyle. You must see yourself whole and complete. You must see yourself completely healed... no longer a drug addict and an abuser of alcohol... but instead, a totally new creation in Christ Jesus. God's CHILD... your mama's child... your Grandpa's precious grand-daughter... a person ready to run to the fight... conquer the enemy and start your life completely in a new place. This is your moment... your opportunity... your new day in God.

Here are some Scriptures to help you in this battle against fear. Interestingly enough, the first one that I have on my heart for you is from Psalm 27 and it was your Grandpa's favorite chapter in the Bible. These are the verses that he read and memorized and quoted on the battlefield in Germany in World War II where he thought he would die. It was on that battlefield that God called him to give up his own dreams of becoming a medical doctor and instead, become a preacher... a pastor... and then years later... a missionary. Take time to memorize these verses... get them down on the inside of you. You have the time to do this. JUST DO IT!

You must meditate on and memorize Scripture so that it is deep within you when you need to share it with someone you will minister to... that needs a verse of Scripture right then as you are talking.

PSALMS 27: 1-6:

"THE LORD IS MY LIGHT AND MY SALVATION; WHOM SHALL I FEAR? THE LORD IS THE DEFENSE OF MY LIFE; WHOM SHALL I DREAD? WHEN EVILDOERS CAME UPON ME TO DEVOUR MY FLESH, MY ADVERSARIES AND MY ENEMIES, THEY STUMBLED AND FELL. THOUGH A HOST ENCAMP AGAINST ME, MY HEART WILL NOT FEAR; THOUGH WAR ARISE AGAINST ME, IN SPITE OF THIS I SHALL BE CONFIDENT. ONE THING I HAVE ASKED FROM THE LORD, THAT I SHALL SEEK: THAT I MAY DWELL IN THE HOUSE OF THE LORD ALL THE DAYS OF MY LIFE, TO BEHOLD THE BEAUTY OF THE LORD, AND TO MEDITATE IN HIS TEMPLE. FOR IN THE DAY OF TROUBLE HE WILL CONCEAL ME IN HIS TABERNACLE; IN THE SECRET PLACE OF HIS TENT HE WILL HIDE ME; HE WILL LIFT ME UP ON A ROCK. AND NOW MY HEAD WILL BE LIFTED UP ABOVE MY ENEMIES AROUND ME. AND I WILL OFFER IN HIS TENT SACRIFICES WITH SHOUTS OF JOY: I WILL SING, YES, I WILL SING PRAISES TO THE LORD."

And then look at the last two verses of that same psalm, Psalm 27:13-14:

"I WOULD HAVE DESPAIRED UNLESS I HAD BELIEVED THAT I WOULD SEE THE GOODNESS OF THE LORD IN THE LAND OF THE LIVING. WAIT FOR THE LORD; BE STRONG, AND LET YOUR HEART TAKE COURAGE; YES, WAIT FOR THE LORD."

And then in John 14: 1-3:

Jesus says this: "LET NOT YOUR HEART BE TROUBLED; BELIEVE IN GOD, BELIEVE ALSO IN ME. IN MY FATHER'S HOUSE ARE MANY DWELLING PLACES, IF IT WERE NOT SO, I WOULD HAVE TOLD YOU; FOR I GO TO PREPARE A PLACE FOR YOU. AND IF I GO AND PREPARE A PLACE FOR YOU, I WILL COME AGAIN, AND RECEIVE YOU TO MYSELF; THAT WHERE I AM, THERE YOU MAY BE ALSO."

So, "let not your heart be troubled"... don't be afraid... don't allow the devil to fill your head with defeating, fearful thoughts.   Run TOWARD the freedom that God has given you through His precious Word. Read it, study it, meditate on it... memorize it! Get it down within you. This is your arsenal against the tricks and schemes that the enemy had planned for you. However, you serve a living God... the one true God... who has wonderful plans for you... plans to bless you and give you a new future... and a new hope! Remember this little song that we used to sing at Cornerstone when you were growing up? We finished our Wednesday night Bible Study with it this week...

I'M SO GLAD THAT JESUS SET ME FREE... I'M SO GLAD THAT JESUS SET ME FREE! I'M SO GLAD THAT JESUS SET ME FREE... SINGING GLORY HALLELUJAH... JESUS SET ME FREE!

SATAN HAD ME BOUND... BUT JESUS SET ME FREE! SATAN HAD ME BOUND, BUT JESUS SET ME FREE... SATAN HAD ME BOUND, BUT JESUS SET ME FREE... SINGING GLORY HALLELUJAH... JESUS SET ME FREE!

I'M ON MY WAY TO HEAVEN AND I'M SHOUTING VICTORY... I'M ON MY WAY TO HEAVEN AND I'M SHOUTING VICTORY... I'M ON MY WAY TO HEAVEN AND I'M SHOUTING VICTORY... SINGING GLORY HALLELUJAH... JESUS SET ME FREE!!!!

Let this become your song. It's a DONE DEAL with God... now just walk in your victory... don't keep your same old thought patterns... give them up to Jesus... let them go... and start seeing yourself as the delivered one... the healed one... the one that is not walking in fear... but instead, WALKS EACH DAY IN VICTORY!

I love you so much, daughter… you can do this… you are doing this… and you are the VICTORIOUS ONE! By the way, that's what your name means… LORI… VICTORIOUS ONE! I had forgotten that… until just this moment as I am typing these words… YOU ARE VICTORIOUS OVER DRUGS, ALCOHOL, CONTROLLING OR ABUSIVE MEN, FALSE FRIENDS AND ALL THE OTHER NEGATIVE IN-FLUENCES UPON YOUR LIFE… ALL OF IT… YES, YOU ARE!

LOVE AND PRAYER SUPPORT FROM… YOUR MOM!

CHAPTER TEN
The Battle is the Lord's!

Dear Lori,

I have so much I want to tell you. I know these letters are long... but they are from my heart. I also know that you are very aware of many of these concepts. Maybe you just haven't seen the need to use them in your daily life. It is true that most people don't begin to really make major life changes until their back is up against a wall... until they really have made a mess of their life in many areas. That seems to be the way a lot of people react. I hope you realize that you are at a point where REAL CHANGE must happen WITHIN you and then carry out in your daily life.

Today I am thinking about roots... where we come from... what makes us who we are... what drives our thought life... all that makes us who we are today.

For so many people, old thinking patterns... maybe stinkin' thinkin', so to speak, is what dictates their everyday life. We are so prone to play again all the "old tapes" in our minds. A lot of these tapes are not good for us. They are the product of past failures and disappointments. They are the results of our "doing it my way"... and "it's really all about me"... All of this is self-centered behavior. It is doing what makes me happy with little or no real concern about how my actions impact all those around me. That type of thinking is prominent in the minds of addicts. They want the momentary pleasure that the drug or alcohol provides... along with the escape. All of this is more important than the consequences of that behavior, which always results in repercussions of some sort or another.

One way to look at this stinkin' thinkin' is that these thought patterns really are your enemies. They do not bring you joy, peace... reassurance of your own self worth and much more. These thoughts bring you down, defeat you and try to get you to wallow in self pity and feelings of insecurity and unworthiness. These thought patterns are your enemies. They are like a huge army of "bad guys" coming at you. They are not good for you... they bring destruction and eventual death.

Do you remember when you were a little girl how you loved to ride your bike around our neighborhood? You and your brothers and all your friends would race around our street that was a huge circle of homes. I remember very clearly one day that as you were racing your bike and talking, you had a serious accident. You did not have your eyes on the road... but instead, you were looking at a friend and talking. Your attention was diverted. As a result, you did not see the huge pothole in the street and as you hit it, you were thrown over your handlebars and you were really hurt. Yes, that accident could have been avoided if you had been paying attention to the road and looked ahead of you to the danger looming in the form of a pothole. Actually, you were hurt so badly that you had a skull fracture. This, of course, kept you from sports and riding your bike for some time.

Daughter, so often our attention is diverted to these feelings that are negative that I've been talking about in this letter. We get sidetracked... caught up in the lies of the devil... and in our own feelings of worthlessness and more, and we fail to see the "potholes" that are right in front of us. We just plow right into them... and then we are really hurt... and so are so many around us. I've been thinking about these enemies and I want to show you some principles found in the book of II Chronicles, chapter 20. This is actually one of my favorite chapters in the Bible and this account is what I preached on at our first service as Beacon of Hope in 2001.

In II Chronicles 20, we find that Jehosophat, the king of Judah, had a report given to him that there was a huge army of warriors coming toward them from a great distance away. Jehosophat was afraid and so he turned his attention to seek the Lord and he gathered all the people of Judah and had them seek the Lord also. I really like verse 12 of that chapter where Jehosophat says this:

"O OUR GOD, WILT THOU NOT JUDGE THEM? FOR WE ARE POWERLESS BEFORE THIS GREAT MULTITUDE WHO ARE COMING AGAINST US, NOR DO WE KNOW WHAT TO DO, BUT OUR EYES ARE ON THEE."

Doesn't that remind you of Step 1... in AA? We are powerless ... we can't fix ourselves... we can't change without the help of Almighty God. Of course, AA says... a higher power. The HIGHEST POWER is God... our loving Heavenly Father. We don't know what to do to make the changes WITHIN us that are needed, do we? That's where the power of God must come in, Lori. That's where true surrender lies. You must give it all up to Him and allow Him to take the cravings and desires for drugs and alcohol away from you. He can and He wants to do just that for you.

The people of Judah saw their need... they knew only God could rescue them from the impending death and destruction that was on the way. They stood before God in prayer and worship. Then the voice of the Lord came to them through the mouth of a prophet, Jahaziel. Beginning in verse 15..."THUS SAYS THE LORD TO YOU, DO NOT FEAR OR BE DISMAYED BECAUSE OF THIS GREAT MULTITUDE, FOR THE BATTLE IS NOT YOURS BUT GOD'S.

TOMORROW GO DOWN AGAINST THEM… FOR THE LORD IS WITH YOU!"

You are not to be afraid, daughter. This battle must be fought by God… for you. What He needs only… is your cooperation… your surrender to His will for you. He will change you. THIS BATTLE IS THE LORD'S! Just let Him fight it for you. You line yourself up with the perfect will of God for your life. You come into agreement with total change of desires and cravings. You surrender all your drug abuse and the habits that come with all of that to God… and watch Him fight the battle for you!

In the next few verses we see that the people began to worship and praise God… even before they saw the victory. I am doing that for you… as are our people at Beacon of Hope. You must also begin to worship, praise and thank God for the total life changes in you before you see them… or even feel them.

In II Chronicles 20:20, Jehosophat says…

"LISTEN TO ME, O JUDAH AND INHABITANTS OF JERUSALEM, PUT YOUR TRUST IN THE LORD YOUR GOD, AND YOU WILL BE ESTABLISHED. PUT YOUR TRUST IN HIS PROPHETS AND SUCCEED."

This is the answer for you. You must put your trust in God and surrender your will and desires to Him and then watch Him do the work in you. I think it's interesting that this verse is 20:20. I think of 20/20 vision when I see that. That is what is considered really good eyesight... 20/20! When you do what that verse says, put your trust completely in God... letting Him do the work in you... you are seeing your situation clearly. You can't change you... but God can do all that needs to be done!

Remember what happened to you when you were not watching the road in front of you? You hit the huge pothole with your bike tire... went over the handlebars...and ended up with a skull fracture. When you trust God completely... especially in this huge problem in your life... He looks ahead for you... you keep your eyes on Him... you trust Him completely...and He goes before you and makes the path straight and clear. He will make a way where there seems to be no way... always remember that.

In verse 21, Jehosophat appointed people to just sing and praise God. They were to sing... "GIVE THANKS TO THE LORD, FOR HIS LOVING KINDESS IS EVERLASTING." In the Message Bible it says this, "GIVE THANKS TO GOD, HIS LOVE NEVER QUITS." That is so wonderful! We know that God loves us and that He never stops loving us... no matter what we have done... so we give thanks to God for the miracles in our lives that have happened and are going to happen!!

Well, the outcome of this story is that as the people began to sing and praise God, God went to work and

He set ambushes against the armies coming toward Judah. The "bad guys" began to fight each other. They literally destroyed EACH OTHER! God had fought the battle for the people of Judah. They looked all around and found a field of dead bodies. All the warriors that were going to come kill them were now dead themselves. No one had escaped. They found so many valuables... clothing, equipment and more that had been left behind. They were truly blessed. When God fights for us... He leaves so much with us... His comfort, His peace, His joy... a knowing deep within us that God has fought this battle for us and will continue to work out all the details that need to be worked out. The blessing of the Lord is working within us... and it's working in you... even now.

Yes, the many valuables that are left behind when we completely turn our lives over to God are amazing. You begin to find that you have a new PEACE down deep within you... that you never recognized before. You find that the EMPTINESS is gone... there is no longer that BIG VOID within. You find that you have a JOY that you can't really explain. There is just something different going on inside of you... It's almost like that excitement on Christmas Eve before we allowed you and your brothers to open your presents on Christmas morning. You knew you were about to receive new things... toys, clothes and more. You knew that there was something wonderful to look forward to. You didn't know exactly what you were getting... but you knew you were going to have surprises... especially things you had asked for and wanted.

It's just like that with God. When we begin to say..."TAKE ME, LORD...CHANGE ME... I SURRENDER TO YOU NOW", something wonderful begins to happen on the inside of us. We are no longer full of doom and gloom and wondering what the next problem will be in our lives... or how we will get that "high"! No, instead a new PEACE moves into the inside of us. God's Holy Spirit begins to do a work in us that we can't do for ourselves. WE SURRENDER... TO WIN!!! We let go of the past and the desires and cravings for all that would bring us down... and He takes over. He pilots the plane of your life.

Look at these words in Proverbs 3:5-6 in the Message Bible: "TRUST GOD FROM THE BOTTOM OF YOUR HEART; DON'T TRY TO FIGURE OUT EVERYTHING ON YOUR OWN. LISTEN FOR GOD'S VOICE IN EVERY-THING YOU DO, EVERYWHERE YOU GO; HE'S THE ONE WHO WILL KEEP YOU ON TRACK."

Remember what Jesus said to us in John 14:27 "PEACE I LEAVE WITH YOU; MY PEACE I GIVE TO YOU; NOT AS THE WORLD GIVES, DO I GIVE TO YOU. LET NOT YOUR HEART BE TROUBLED, NOR LET IT BE FEARFUL."

Take the peace that God has for you. Rest in His capable arms and allow Him to fight this battle for you. He is setting you free from years of drug abuse. Just know that He loves you so much that He will do a complete work in you. You have plenty of time now....your attention should be on recovery. YOU ARE BEING HEALED FROM ALL OF THE PAIN OF YOUR LIFE OF DRUGS. You are going to begin to experience more peace and comfort than you have ever known. This really is your new day! I am singing praises to God for the work He has been doing... and will continue to do in you, my daughter.

Always remember how very much you are loved by your family and friends... and especially how much God, your heavenly Father, loves you!

All is well!
YOUR MOM

Marcia McAllister

CHAPTER ELEVEN
Going the Distance

Good morning Lori,

I am at my desk again...very early... beginning to write to you.   This is all somewhat surreal for me... not being able to talk to you but having the ability to pour out my feelings and desires for you on paper. Most parents probably never experience something quite like this. Life seems to keep everyone so busy these days. There are so many demands for our time and attention that perhaps most people don't ever have the experience of writing to a child in such detail.

Actually, I am grateful to God for this experience. It is really helping me put your situation in proper perspective and giving me renewed insight into you and what God desires for your life.   As I have been praying so much for you, I really do see you coming out of this experience a completely different person. I trust our wonderful Lord that He is causing you to see the changes you need to make and that deep, definite decisions are being made in you that will forever change the course of your life. I also believe that so many other families will be touched by your story and that perhaps some people somewhere will make life changing decisions from this account of the years of suffering that you... and your family... have experienced as a result of your drug abuse.

I am reminded this morning of the brevity of life. Yesterday after church some of us were standing around talking about our ages. We all agreed that we really don't seem to see ourselves at the age we really are. Deep within us we still feel much younger... and it seems even odd to us that we are the ages we have become. A couple of our people are now in their late eighties and seventies... that seems almost impossible. This week we celebrated your Grandma's eighty-sixth birthday. I can still picture her and Grandpa at their young ages of "thirty something". I also am remembering Grandpa's funeral and the beautiful video that your Aunt Karen and Uncle Myron put together of his life. What a joy to see all the pictures of him as a little boy....and then progressively throughout the years. As each of the grandchildren were added to the family....and then now all the seventeen great grandchildren, it really is amazing to see the progression of time and how all of our lives are intertwined together. There were so many pictures of fun family times together...especially with your Grandpa. What a fun, joyful person he was!

And so, all of that brings me to what I want to talk to you about today.   I am reminded of you as a little girl and all the fun times you had in your early years. You were busy playing T-ball on a little league team when you were five.   Starting in fourth grade, you tried out and made the cheerleading squad at school. You actually were a cheerleader for several years. I can still picture you out there on the basketball floor in your green and white outfit. You were great at cheerleading and you seemed to always have a wonderful time at the games.

I can also see you running track. Remember that? You seemed to really enjoy that sport a lot. All of those times seem so long ago... don't they?   They did happen. You were very involved with fun activities and sports. You loved to go to the middle school games with your friends. You loved to cheer your brothers on with their basketball and baseball games. All that was a big part of your life at that age. Then all of our lives began to change... ever so slowly at first... but they definitely did change, didn't they?

I must say that you always did seem to have that rebellious side to you.   Even though you seemed to conform to the norm of most of your friends, you were continually pushing to get your own way and do what you wanted to do... when you wanted to do it.   I remember many battles with you over situations where you were not where you were supposed to be at a given time... or where you were not home when you were supposed to be. I also remember many times of catching you in lies and all the arguments that followed all of that. I know that this is all very common in homes with teenagers. However, something began to change when you began to hang around some kids that were much different than you. Actually, it seemed that you developed an attraction for all the troubled kids. Instead of your cheerleader friends, for instance... you began to want to spend time with kids who seemed to constantly be in trouble. You appeared to really be attracted to boys who were prone to fights and suspensions at school. I remember so many times that your big brother, Ryan, would try to talk to you about all of this... only to have you dismiss his concern for you. His advice and warnings to you went unheeded... and you continued to associate with people who seemed to always contribute to your rebellious behavior.

I can't say exactly when you began to experiment with drugs and alcohol, but I do know that it was during your high school years. Your goals and desires seemed to change. You were becoming a different person right before our eyes. I remember many attempts to talk to you about the troubled friends... and times of your drinking... and probably using drugs. Those talks... even family talks... seemed to go nowhere. You were on a path... a path of "doing your own thing"... a path of rebellion and no one was going to be able to stop all of that... but you!

And you chose to continue to live a lifestyle of drinking and drugging.   You were accepted into Indiana University and went there as a freshman with so much potential. You had a nice roommate... and you told how you liked your classes and were studying a lot.   However, there was really more to that story.   Your drinking and partying got the best of you and you flunked out after only one semester. Actually, we all know that you had the ability to do very well in college... but you chose the OTHER PATH... the one of self-destruction and defeat.   You were going to have a "good time" in life... do your own thing... not be told what to do... or what was good for you.   You went back to our hometown and you continued to live a lifestyle of drug abuse and drinking.

This lifestyle soon had you living with a young man who you said you loved so much. You have often said that Eric introduced you to so many drugs and experiences that continued to make your habits stronger.   I have no doubt about that... but again, you CHOSE that lifestyle with him and his friends. We know where he is now... in prison for a very long time.

It was during that time of your life, that I first convinced you to come down to Florida and live with me and let me help you get on the right track.   Do you remember all of that?   The event that prompted that move was you being physically... and emotionally... BEAT UP by this man.   Your jaw was dislocated... you were bruised and beaten... by this man who you loved so much. Your Grandpa Jay actually drove you down here in your car that he had given you. Your intentions were to stay here for awhile and get a job and get some much needed outpatient drug rehab.

We actually had an appointment the night you arrived here with a wonderful counseling center. Remember Deb? She has continued to be a friend to me through the years and has helped me deal with your addiction and my co-dependency... long after you bolted from that program. You were able to get a good job at Chili's Restaurant... right near my real estate office. I remember going to some sessions with you at the counseling center. I was very concerned about your attitude. You seemed to not take any of this very seriously at all. You were still recovering from your injuries inflicted on you by Eric... when you suddenly decided to run away in your little red car and head back to Indiana. I think you were only here for about 4-5 weeks during that stay.

I remember that day like it was yesterday. I was at work and received a call from Chili's asking why you hadn't showed up for your shift. Of course, I was not able to reach you on the phone at home. One of my friends in my office, Jim... who had been talking to you and trying to help you... drove with me as I hurried home to see about you. Yes, you were gone... all of your belongings were taken with you... and the note was on the kitchen counter. It was short and to the point... yes, you had gone back to Eric... you loved him... and it would all be alright again.

Now, me being the co-dependent mother that I was... at that time... did the only reasonable thing to do, didn't I? I ended up going to the airport... did not pack a bag... just got on a plane and flew to Memphis. Why Memphis? Well, you had called from the road as you stopped near Memphis to tell me that you wanted to come back to Florida and stay in the rehab. You had changed your mind. Would I come get you and drive you back here? You weren't feeling good and were worried about the drive back to Florida. I gave my credit card information to the hotel front desk where you were and you promised to stay there until I could get to you. I then boarded a plane to Memphis. Somewhere up in the air, I began to realize what was really going on here. I wondered if you would still be at the hotel when I got there. As soon as I landed, I called the man at the front desk that I had been talking to just a couple of hours before.

Why was Lori not answering the phone in her room, I asked. Well, he had watched her exit the parking lot to go get something to eat. But, he had seen her get on the interstate going north, instead of pulling into the restaurant nearby... and she had not returned. Yes, Lori was now on the road to Indiana... and where was I? At the airport in Memphis...with a decision to make. Again, being the co-dependent mother that I was... at that time... (sound familiar?) ... I bought an expensive ticket to Indianapolis and ran the distance of the airport to get to my plane that was already boarding. Yes, I went to Indiana... rented a car... all the time calculating how long it would take you to get to a certain crossroads near our hometown.   Of course, I was praying that I would be able to beat you to that intersection... stop you and convince you to come back home with me to Florida!!! Oh, my! I made so many mistakes in all of that trip and yes, it cost me a whole lot of money to make that effort at rescuing you... yet one more time.

I remember standing at a pay phone on the corner by your apartment that you shared with Eric. Your car was parked there. It was now snowing... I had no coat with me. I had left sunny Florida only a few hours before.   I called and called you. I left you messages. I banged on your door... only to hear very loud music coming from that apartment. You did not respond to any of my pleadings.   I went to your brother Ryan's home... stayed all night and then boarded another plane and headed back to Florida. What a big lesson I had learned... once again.   It's very hard to rescue someone who doesn't want to be res cued... especially if they have decided not to go along with the rescue!!

Unfortunately, Lori, we have had so many situations throughout the years where different ones of your family and friends have tried so hard to get you into drug rehab centers... only to have you walk out within a few days or even a few hours of your arrival there. Yes, we have all been trying our best to rescue you from the life of drug and alcohol abuse that you have lived for almost twenty years. We are aware of the attempts that we have made to help you... and we are very aware of your response to that help.

All of that has brought us to this point in time where you are now sentenced to prison for an extended period of time. Interventions of one type or another by so many of us have really not caused you to see the effects of your life of drugs. Yes, we have all had such good intentions but perhaps you were not really ready to completely change and choose a new life for yourself. Maybe the changes we have all wanted for you, have really been our desires... and not yours at all. At least that is how all of this appears at this time. I do believe, with all my heart, that this moment in time can be your major point of change. This can be the time that you forever give up the lifestyle you have lived for so long. It will definitely take work on your part. When the thoughts of going back to your old life seem to monopolize your thoughts, you will have to choose to change your thinking and remember all the pain and agony that the life of drug abuse has truly brought you. Has it been worth all that you have suffered? I hope the answer is a resounding **NO**... to you... because that is definitely the answer for all of us that love you so much.

Today I am reminded of some words in the book of Colossians in chapter three, beginning in verse 3 in the Message Bible...

"YOUR OLD LIFE IS DEAD. YOUR NEW LIFE, WHICH IS YOUR REAL LIFE—EVEN THOUGH INVISIBLE TO SPECTATORS---IS WITH CHRIST IN GOD. HE IS YOUR LIFE...

Going on down to verse 5 of Colossians 3,

"AND THAT MEANS KILLING OFF EVERYTHING CONNECTED WITH THAT WAY OF DEATH: SEXUAL PROMISCUITY, IMPURITY, LUST, DOING WHATEVER YOU FEEL LIKE WHENEVER YOU FEEL LIKE IT, AND GRABBING WHATEVER ATTRACTS YOUR FANCY. THAT'S A LIFE SHAPED BY THINGS AND FEELINGS INSTEAD OF BY GOD...

BUT YOU KNOW BETTER NOW, SO MAKE SURE IT'S ALL GONE FOR GOOD; BAD TEMPER, IRRITABILITY, MEANNESS, PROFANITY, DIRTY TALK. DON'T LIE TO ONE ANOTHER...

This passage of Scripture is so "right on" for you, Lori. I hope you will take the time to really read and study the whole chapter. Starting again at verse 12 of Colossians 3...

"SO, CHOSEN BY GOD FOR THIS NEW LIFE OF LOVE, DRESS IN THE WARD-ROBE GOD PICKED

OUT FOR YOU: COMPASSION, KINDNESS, HUMILITY, QUIET STRENGTH, DISCIPLINE. BE EVEN-TEMPERED, CONTENT WITH SECOND PLACE, QUICK TO FORGIVE AN OFFENSE. FORGIVE AS QUICKLY AND COMPLETELY AS THE MASTER FOR-GAVE YOU. AND REGARDLESS OF WHAT ELSE YOU PUT ON, WEAR LOVE. IT'S YOUR BASIC, ALL –PURPOSE GARMENT. NEVER BE WITHOUT IT. LET THE PEACE OF CHRIST KEEP YOU IN TUNE WITH EACH OTHER, IN STEP WITH EACH OTHER. NONE OF THIS GOING OFF AND DOING YOUR OWN THING. CULTIVATE THANKFULNESS."

Now that is specific direction, isn't it? There's no doubt what the apostle Paul was talking about here. He is giving instruction on exactly how to conduct ourselves. This is so very important. He goes on in that chapter to talk about the importance of the Word of God in our lives. It's His Word that will teach you exactly the things you must change. This passage is really a good place to start as you sincerely begin to evaluate your past life and decide how you want to live in the future.

God is speaking very clearly to you here. I hope you see the importance of all of this and actually begin to change your attitudes accordingly.

Have you ever heard of the program… INTERVENTION? It's on a cable channel and it deals with families like ours that have a person in the family that is severely drug addicted. They show in detail the agony that the family goes through... the pleading with the addict to change... and the actual time of intervention when they all sit down and share their feelings. It is painful to watch as these family members pour out their feelings to the addict. Often everyone involved is crying and sometimes sobbing as they tell their story of the effects of all the drug abuse on each of them.

All of this brings me to the subject of your precious ten year old son, Levi. Yes, your Dad and his family... and all of my family, including your brothers and your sister in law, niece and nephews and of course, me... have been greatly affected by your years of drug and alcohol abuse. However, as great an effect as that has been on all of us, I have to wonder if you have really been that aware of the issues that Levi has faced through these years of his life.

I know you love him so very much. I have seen that... I have felt your agony when you cannot see him... talk to him very often... or be a part of his daily life. Yes, I know that all of the separation from him hurts you very deeply. But, Lori, this relationship between you and your son is so much more than just being there for him when he comes home from school. I want you to allow yourself to think about this separation and feel the feelings that are lodged there deep within you.

I think this is a very good time for you to ask the Lord to show you how your addictions have hurt your son. So many countless times you have chosen the "high"... the evening of drug use... or even days of it... over time with your son. This has been such a way of life for you that you may not even be aware of the backseat that Levi has had to take in your life... to your drug habit. Good parenting involves caring about the feelings of our children. It involves us, as parents, trying our best to live in such a way that our children are not resentful of us or our decisions. Being a good mother has so much to do with the values and life lessons we pass down to our kids. They learn these lessons by what they see in us... much more so than what we say.

You have a perfect opportunity right now to show your son just how very much you do love him. This will be accomplished by you taking the time to really look at your past decisions where he is concerned. What have all your years of drug abuse gotten you? Certainly you would not want Levi to grow up and become a drug addict or alcoholic, would you? The answer has to be NO, doesn't it? You wouldn't want that life for your son or your future grandchildren. With that said, it is time NOW... this special time in your life... to look at your past decisions and feel the feelings that are buried deep within you where the relationship with your son is concerned. Don't be afraid to feel... own the feelings of regret, shame and hurt... and then allow the Lord to begin the healing process in you where those awful feelings are concerned.

I know you have memories of so many times that he has seen you 'all messed up' on drugs. I know he has heard things come from your mouth that he shouldn't have had to hear. I also feel that there is a sadness deep within him where you are concerned. He wants you to be the mommy who is there for him... who is the parent, loving him and taking care of him. He does love you so very much... and always will. There is still time, daughter, to make all this right with him. It really does start with facing your mistakes... the disappointments and hurtful actions that have happened to him.

As you know, I had Levi with me this summer for about three weeks. We had a wonderful time together. We went to ball games, swam a lot, watched our Rays on TV almost every day... hung out together with family and our church friends. It was all such a great time. Everyone loves him so much. He has your wonderful humor ... is so bright... so quick to understand. I thoroughly enjoyed this special time with my grandson. I only wish you could have been with us. He really does miss you so much. He looks forward to the time when you will be released from prison and he can be with you again.

With all that said, he really can't bear to talk much about where you are... and what your life must be like in there. It hurts him so much to think about it.

So, this is another important part of your recovery. You must face the results of your drug and alcohol addictions. You must allow God to show you the depth of the problem. You must take the time to do the "step work" in your recovery program and feel the feelings that are buried deep within you. I can't tell you what to feel... or even how to change those feelings... but I do know that the power of Almighty God is there within you to guide you into this recovery. God's Holy Spirit will show you events, times of serious misconduct that have hurt Levi deeply, and the seriousness of this addiction and how you can completely come out of it. Forgive yourself... determine to give all that past life up forever... and move into all that God has for you to do. This includes becoming the mother that he wants you to be. You can do it, daughter. I know you can.

I am reminded of the words of Paul in Romans 12:1-2 "I URGE YOU THEREFORE, BRETHREN, BY THE MERCIES OF GOD, TO PRESENT YOUR BODIES A LIVING AND HOLY SACRIFICE, ACCEPTABLE TO GOD, WHICH IS YOUR SPIRITUAL SERVICE OF WORSHIP. AND DO NOT BE CON-FORMED TO THIS WORLD, BUT BE TRANSFORMED BY THE RENEWING OF YOUR MIND, THAT YOU MANY PROVE WHAT THE WILL OF GOD IS, THAT WHICH IS GOOD AND ACCEPTABLE AND PERFECT."

This is found in the New American Standard Bible and is the wording I memorized so many years ago.

It's time to renew your mind... to God's perfect will for your life. Since I have been teaching for awhile now out of the modern language translation of the Bible, the Message Bible... I want you to see the wording of these two verses in our everyday language.

"SO HERE'S WHAT I WANT YOU TO DO, GOD HELPING YOU: TAKE YOUR EVERYDAY, ORDINARY LIFE--- YOUR SLEEPING, EATING, GOING-TO-WORK, AND WALKING-AROUND LIFE---AND PLACE IT BEFORE GOD AS AN OFFERING. EMBRACING WHAT GOD DOES FOR YOU IS THE BEST THING YOU CAN DO FOR HIM. DON'T BECOME SO WELL-ADJUSTED TO YOUR CULTURE THAT YOU FIT INTO IT WITHOUT EVEN THINKING. INSTEAD, FIX YOUR ATTENTION ON GOD. YOU'LL BE CHANGED FROM THE INSIDE OUT. READILY RECOGNIZE WHAT HE WANTS FROM YOU, AND QUICKLY RESPOND TO IT. UNLIKE THE CULTURE AROUND YOU, ALWAYS DRAGGING YOU DOWN TO ITS LEVEL OF IMMATURITY, GOD BRINGS THE BEST OUT OF YOU, DEVELOPS WELL-FORMED MATURITY IN YOU."

Oh, I love all of that. It really tells us what to do to develop the maturity that we all need. We give God our ordinary lives. We realize that we can live a better life than we have lived...with His help and His intervention. We begin to see what He wants for us...and we quickly respond to His leading. God develops us into who He created us to be...and we learn to GO THE DISTANCE... with Him leading us each day! We refuse to just exist... just live the way we always have lived. Instead, we make a quality decision to change forever... to indeed,

GO THE DISTANCE with Him!

And one day we will leave this earthly realm... and go the total distance... to our place already prepared for us in heaven.

Jesus said in John 14:1-3
"LET NOT YOUR HEART BE TROUBLED: BELIEVE IN GOD, BELIEVE ALSO IN ME. IN MY FATHER'S HOUSE ARE MANY DWELLING PLACES, IF IT WERE NOT SO, I WOULD HAVE TOLD YOU; FOR I GO TO PREPARE A PLACE FOR YOU. AND IF I GO AND PREPARE A PLACE FOR YOU, I WILL COME AGAIN, AND RECEIVE YOU TO MYSELF, THAT WHERE I AM, THERE YOU MAY BE ALSO."

So, we have a purpose... we have goals, we have a plan for our lives. All of that is individually shown to us by our loving heavenly Father. Find all of that, Lori, in God. Talk to Him... tell Him how you feel... confess the sin, the mistakes, the poor judgment, all of it....to Him. He is right there ready to forgive you... ready to speak to you and show you the new path you must be on... and the path that will allow you to GO THE DISTANCE with Him working in you. It is only then that your life will take on the true meaning that God ordained for you to accomplish.

And those are my thoughts this day... please know that I love you so very much and have utmost confidence in you that you can do this... you can recover from your drug addiction... you can be the ambassador for God that He has called you to be. You can change lives of people around you that have some of the same problems that you have had. You can bring light and life to lost ones all around you. Yes, you can do all this, my daughter... because the living God... the all powerful God... the all knowing and all loving God... your God... lives in you and wants to totally change you... from the inside out! Just let Him do it!

Your MOM... who is always here for you... because I love you!

CHAPTER TWELVE
If We Could Only See

August 27, 2010

Dear Reader,

I began the writing of this book on May 3, 2010. Lori was given her prison sentence on April 28, 2010. The words just flowed out of me in such a powerful way that I can only attribute this work to the power of God... giving me the words and concepts to write. I never had an outline of what needed to be communicated about my daughter, Lori. God just reminded me of stories about her... gave me His insight as I wrote... and brought it all together into this manuscript.

I actually wrote the whole book within the month of May... except for the last half of the last chapter, that was written today. I had to take a break from writing in late May due to the acquisition of a new church building for the congregation that I pastor in Clearwater, Florida. Since it was brand new, we had a lot of work to do to get it ready to occupy. We celebrated this new move of God in our ministry on August 1...just a few weeks ago. All of that work and excitement is now behind us and we move on with the calling of God to reach as many as we can with the love and mercy of the Lord.

I did take a trip to Indiana in June to spend time with my four precious grandchildren and my son, Ryan and his wife, Elizabeth. We had such a great time going to the kid's ball games and just enjoying being together. Early one morning I picked up Lori's son, Levi and we headed out to come back to Florida. As I wrote in the last chapter, we had a wonderful time together. He is a very sweet, intelligent and entertaining young man... and he does love his mommy so much.

I have now been able to talk to Lori several times since mid June. She is housed in a minimum security prison in Indiana and is a part of a drug abuse recovery unit within that facility. This is a good opportunity for her to work on her recovery. I have sent her several of these letters...and we are communicating about insight she is receiving from them. She did go through several weeks of "boot camp" before entering the facility where she now is, which proved to be very difficult for her. All in all, she is beginning to adjust to this very different life. It is not easy for her... there are many issues that arise.

For the past two weeks she has been fighting a serious staph infection that she acquired there in the facility. She has been very ill and is finally beginning to feel better in the past few days. As you can imagine, she has many difficult times and is always so happy to hear from a family member or friend.

If I could see ahead... I would want to see my daughter totally changed forever. Do I believe that this can happen? Absolutely. I know that this is God's will for her. I know that she can work on all these issues and finally get the proper perspective on her addictions and her past life

Since I can't exactly see what lies ahead... I choose to believe that she will learn from all of that she has experienced and that she will allow God to work in her life in a new way. My prayer is that she will take these chapters and allow the Holy Spirit to speak to her heart... teaching her what she needs to learn about herself... and about His wonderful nature. I pray that she will so want to change that she will do the work it takes to move forward into her new way of life... with the drug addictions behind her. I also choose to believe that God will somehow use Lori's life story to help countless others who are struggling with these same issues. Also, may these words help family members and friends receive HOPE for the similar problems that they may be encountering with a loved one.

In conclusion, the words of the Apostle Paul found in Ephesians 3: 14-20 from the Message Bible translation are my prayer for you this day...

"MY RESPONSE IS TO GET DOWN ON MY KNEES BEFORE THE FATHER, THIS MAGNIFICENT FATHER WHO PARCELS OUT ALL HEAVEN AND EARTH. I ASK HIM TO STRENGTHEN YOU BY HIS SPIRIT—NOT A BRUTE STRENGTH BUT A GLORIOUS INNER STRENGTH—THAT CHRIST WILL LIVE IN YOU AS YOU OPEN THE DOOR AND INVITE HIM IN. AND I ASK HIM THAT WITH BOTH FEET PLANTED FIRMLY ON LOVE, YOU'LL BE ABLE TO TAKE IN WITH ALL FOLLOWERS OF JESUS THE EXTRAVA-GANT DIMENSIONS OF CHRIST'S LOVE. REACH OUT AND EXPERIENCE THE BREADTH! TEST ITS LENGTH! PLUMB THE DEPTHS! RISE TO THE HEIGHTS! LIVE FULL LIVES, FULL IN THE FULLNESS OF GOD.

GOD CAN DO ANYTHING, YOU KNOW – FAR MORE THAN YOU COULD EVER IMAGINE OR GUESS OR REQUEST IN YOUR WILDEST DREAMS! HE DOES IT NOT BY PUSHING US AROUND BUT BY WORKING WITHIN US, HIS SPIRIT DEEPLY AND GENTLY WITHIN US."

May God richly bless your life.
In His love and for His glory,
Marcia McAllister

LORI LYNN McALLISTER

,

Made in United States
Orlando, FL
07 November 2021